The Children Act 1989

in the context of
The Human Rights Act
1998

Fergus Smith

B.Sc.(Hons), M.A., C.Q.S.W., D.M.S., Dip.M

Professor Tina Lyon

LL.B, FRSA, Queen Victoria Professor of Law, Solicitor of the Supreme Court
and Director of the Centre for t~~...~~
Law at the University of Liverpo~~...~~

Children Act Enterprises Ltd (CAE)
103 Mayfield Road
South Croydon
Surrey CR2 0BH

www.caeuk.org

© Fergus Smith 2006

British Library Cataloguing in Publication Data
A catalogue record for this book is available from the
British Library

ISBN 1-899986-27-8

Designed and typeset by Andrew Haig & Associates
Printed in the UK by The Lavenham Press

CAE is an independent organisation which publishes
guides to family and criminal law and provides
consultancy, research, training and independent
investigation services to the public, private and voluntary
sectors.

Contents

Appendices

Regulations are 'subordinate' legislation which must be obeyed.

'Guidance' is Government advice which does not have the force of law, but should be complied with unless local circumstances indicate exceptional reasons which justify a variation.

'Public law' refers to services the State provides for families and the procedures followed by the State to protect children when families fail to do so. 'Private law' is concerned with the allocation of responsibility/ resolution of disputes between parents and/or other individuals.

Where case law is referred to:
All ER = All England Law Reports
EHRR = European Human Rights Reports
Fam. = Official law reports: Family Division of High Court
Fam. Law = Family Law
FCR = Family Court Reports
FLR = Family Law Reports

Other abbreviations used:
ECHR = European Convention for the Protection of
Human Rights and Fundamental Freedoms
CPA 2004 = Civil Partnership Act 2004
CA 2004 = Children Act 2004
ACA 2002 = Adoption and Children Act 2002
CAA 2006 = Children and Adoption Act 2006
CA 1989 = Children Act 1989
FLRA 1987 = Family Law Reform Act 1987

All references, unless otherwise stated, are to the
Children Act 1989.

The text reflects statute as at 01.09.06 (insofar as
Commencement Orders have been issued) and the most
significant reported case law as at 01.04.06.

Introduction

- This guide is designed for use by all those in England and Wales who work with children and their families.

- It aims to provide easy access to, and reinforce understanding of the main messages of the Children Act 1989, including the most significant case law.

- A comprehensive summary of the Children (Leaving Care) Act 2000, consequent regulations and their interface with the Children Act 1989 is included.

- The guide also reflects the implications of the Care Standards Act 2000, Adoption and Children Act 2002, Carers and Disabled Children Act 2000, Civil Partnership Act 2004 and the (yet to be implemented) Children and Adoption Act 2006.

- The guide should be used only to supplement government regulations, guidance and local policies and procedures.

- Appendix 1 provides a summary of relevant Articles and Protocols of the European Convention on Human Rights and appendix 2 is a summary of the Human Rights Act 1998 which brought the provisions of the Convention into UK law on 02.10.00

- The significant impact of the Convention on the Children Act is noted at relevant places throughout the text.

Key Points

■ The child's welfare is paramount and safeguarding and promoting it is the priority.

  NB. It has been suggested that this may conflict with parents' rights under Article 8(1) of the Convention which provides for the right to respect for family life [Hendriks v Netherlands [1982] 5 EHRR 223].

  Others conclude that paramountcy is consistent with Convention case-law, within the 'margin of appreciation' permitted national authorities under Article 8(2) and therefore compatible with the right to respect for family life [Lord Hobhouse in Dawson v Wearmouth [1999] in FLR 167 who stated that 'there is nothing in the Convention which requires the courts of this country to act otherwise than in accordance with the interests of the child'].

  LJ Butler-Sloss in the Court of Appeal stated that where there was a conflict of interest between the rights and interests of a child and those of a parent, the interests of the child had to prevail under Article 8(2) of the European Convention [Re L, V, M and H [2000] FLR 334]

■ Local authorities have a duty to ensure that support services for 'children in need' are provided and should minimise unnecessary intrusion into family life.

■ Delay in resolution of court proceedings and provision of service must be avoided.

NB. This principle received further reinforcement by the incorporation of Article 6 of the Convention which provides for the right to a fair trial within a reasonable time [see below for further discussion].

■ Service providers must listen to and work in partnership with children and parents, any who have parental responsibility and relevant others.

■ Needs arising from race, culture, religion and language must be taken into account by service providers and courts.

Concepts & Principles

Civil Partnership

The Civil Partnership Act 2004 (CPA 2004) introduced into English law the concept of the 'civil partnership'.

S.1 CPA 2004 thus provides that 'a civil partnership' is a relationship between 2 same-sex 'civil partners' formed when they register as civil partners of each other in England and Wales under Part 2 of the Act.

Thus, this allows, for the first time in UK law, that official legal recognition of the relationship of same sex couples can be accorded, provided the couple has registered the relationship under the provisions of CPA 2004.

NB. The term can therefore only be used to refer to partners who have so registered.

Family [s.17]

- For purposes of providing support services, the term family includes any person with parental responsibility and anyone with whom the child has been living.

Looked After [s.22]

- Children who are 'looked after' by a local authority may be 'accommodated', 'in care' or 'remanded/detained'.

- Accommodation is a voluntary arrangement under

which the local authority does not gain parental responsibility and no notice is required for removal of the child.

■ 'In care' means that a court has made a child subject of a Care Order which gives the local authority parental responsibility and (some) authority to limit parents' exercise of their continuing parental responsibility.

■ The local authority has specific authority to detain those who fall into the 3rd category (though with the exception of Emergency Protection Orders, does not gain parental responsibility) who may do so because of a:

- Remand by a court following criminal charges
- Detention following arrest by police
- Emergency Protection or Child Assessment Order
- 'Criminal' Supervision Order with a residence requirement

NB. S.22 (1) (b) as amended by s.2 Children (Leaving Care) Act 2000 enables the local authority to provide accommodation for a child who has left its care without her/him being considered 'looked after'.

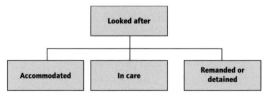

Local Authority [s.105]

- Means County Council, Metropolitan District, London Borough and Unitary Authorities, not just a particular Department.

No Delay Principle [s.1(2)]

- In all court proceedings, delay is presumed to be prejudicial, though this presumption can be rebutted if the delay is a constructive one [Re B (A Minor) (Contact) (Interim Order) 1994 2 FLR].

  NB. See also Article 6 of the Convention (Right To A Fair Trial).

Paramountcy Principle [s.1 (1)]

- When a court determines any question with respect to a child's upbringing or administration of property or income, her/his welfare must be the paramount consideration.

- In cases where the s.1 (1) criteria apply and the interests of two or more children conflict, it is for the court to reach a decision based on a balancing exercise [see dicta of Balcombe LJ in Birmingham City Council v H (No.2) 1 FLR 883 1993].

- The House of Lords has confirmed that where both parent and child are 'children' within the meaning of the Act, the child's needs are paramount [Birmingham City Council v H (No.2) [1993]1 FLR 883 HL].

- It has been accepted by the Court of Appeal that a Parental Responsibility Order relates to the upbringing of a child so is governed by the paramountcy principle [Re G (A Minor) (Parental Responsibility Order) [1994] 1 FLR 504] and the A (Conjoined Twins) [2001] FLR].

- Lord Hobhouse in Dawson v Wearmouth and the Court of Appeal in Re L, V, M and H (see p. 2) indicate the paramountcy principle can be read into Article 8(2) which provides the qualifications for interference with the rights laid down in Article 8(1).

Parental Responsibility [s.3]

- Parental responsibility means all the rights, duties, powers, responsibilities and authority which by law a parent has in relation to a child and her/his property.

  NB. The notion of parental rights is reinforced and given renewed emphasis by Article 8(1) of the Convention.

  Current provisions for allocation and acquisition of parental responsibility are explained below and reflect the changes introduced by the Adoption and Children Act 2002 and Civil Partnership Act 2004.

Positive Advantage [s.1 (5)]

- A court cannot make any order unless it considers to do so would be better than making no order.

Welfare Checklist [s.1 (3)]

■ If considering an opposed s.8 Order or Care or
Supervision Orders (including Interim Care and
Supervision and Education Supervision Orders), the
court must have regard to checklist of:

- Child's wishes/feelings
- Physical, emotional, educational needs
- Likely effect of change of circumstances
- Age, sex, background, relevant characteristics
  (this should include race, culture, religion and
  language)
- Actual or potential harm
- Capability of parents/relevant others to meet
  child's needs
- Available range of powers

■ Although the child's wishes and feelings appear first,
they have no priority over others included in the
welfare checklist [Re W (A Minor) (Medical
Treatment): Court's Jurisdiction) [1993] 1 FLR 1].

*NB. In s.4 applications for Parental Responsibility
Orders the court does not have to apply the statutory
criteria of s.1 (3) and (4) but both court and parties
ought to bear these criteria in mind where they may
be relevant e.g. strongly expressed wishes of an older
child.*

Part 1: Parental Responsibility

Parental Responsibility

Allocation in Case of Married Parents

■ Where a child's parents were married to each other at any time following her/his conception they each have parental responsibility [s.2(1) & s.1 FLRA 1987].

■ The Children Act 1989 emphasises the enduring nature of married parents' responsibility towards their child/ren which can be lost only if s/he is freed for adoption, adopted, attains the age of 18 or dies.

■ Each parent/other person with parental responsibility can act independently in the exercise of it e.g. giving consent to medical treatment.

NB. In Re J (Specific Issue Order: Child's Religious Upbringing and Circumcision) 2000 1 FLR, Thorpe LJ and Dame Butler Sloss P in the Court of Appeal agreed there was a small group of important or exceptional decisions which ought not to be carried out without consent of all those who have parental responsibility, or a court.

Case law suggests these are irreversible actions e.g. circumcision and sterilisation but also includes: immunisation against infectious diseases [see Re C [2003] 2FLR 1095] changes of surname [see Re S [2001] 2 FLR 1005] or school or type of education [see Re P [2003] 1 FLR 286, in which the Court of

Appeal emphasised courts must not abdicate from their duty to decide such matters where parents cannot agree.

Allocation in Case of Civil Partners

■ Where a child's parent (parent A) who has parental responsibility for the child is a civil partner of a person who is **not** the child's parent i.e. is a step-parent:

- Parent A (or if the other parent also has parental responsibility, both parents) may by agreement with the step-parent provide for her/him to have parental responsibility for the child [s.4A(1)(a)] or
- The court may, on the application of the step-parent, order that s/he has parental responsibility for the child [s.4A(1)(b) introduced by s.112 ACA 2002 and amended by s.75 CPA 2004]

NB. The CPA 2004 amended the definitions in s.105 (1) Children Act 1989 so that a 'child of the family' means with respect to those who are civil partners, a child of both of them, and any other child (other than one placed with them as foster carers by a local authority or voluntary organisation) who has been treated by them as a child of their family.

Divorce/ Dissolution of Civil Partnership

■ If a married couple separate or divorce, both

continue to have parental responsibility for their child/ren.

■ Similarly, a couple in a registered civil partnership who have parental responsibility and separate or dissolve the partnership also retain parental responsibility.

■ Such couples are expected to agree suitable arrangements and court orders to determine with whom the child/ren should live, have contact or other related matters will only be made when necessary.

NB. A parent divorced prior to implementation of the Children Act 1989 and not awarded 'custody', gained parental responsibility on 14.10.91 when the Act was implemented. S/he may not exercise this parental responsibility in any way which is inconsistent with any order a court originally or subsequently made.

Allocation in Case of Unmarried Woman & Man

■ Where a child's mother and father were not married to each other at any time following her/his conception:

- The mother has parental responsibility for the child [s.2(2)(a)] and
- The father will have parental responsibility if he has acquired it and has not ceased to have it [s.2(2)(b) as amended by s.111 ACA 2002]

Acquisition of Parental Responsibility by Unmarried Father [s.4 as amended by s.111 ACA 2002]

- s.4 has been amended by s.111 (1)–(3) ACA 2002 to allow an unmarried father to obtain parental responsibility, if:

  - He registers as the child's father in England and Wales under specified sections of the Births and Deaths Registration Act 1953 (or their equivalents in Scotland and Northern Ireland) [s.4(1)(a) CA 1989]

  NB. For all children born after 01.12.03 where the father jointly registered the birth with the mother, he will have acquired automatic parental responsibility; for those children born before 01.12.03 even where the father registered the birth jointly with the mother he will have to take positive steps to acquire such responsibility either by seeking re-registration under the terms of the Births and Deaths Registration Act 1953 or under the provisions of s.4 CA 1989]

  - He and the child's mother make a 'parental responsibility agreement' providing for him to have parental responsibility for the child [s.4(1)(b) CA 1989] or
  - The court, on his application, orders that he shall have parental responsibility for the child [s.4(1) (c) CA 1989

  NB. An unmarried father could also acquire parental responsibility if the child's mother had appointed him in her will as the child's guardian, and subsequently died [s.5 (6) CA 1989].

■ A person who has acquired parental responsibility as above, ceases to have it only if [s.4(2A) as substituted by s.111(4) ACA 2002] the court so orders on the application of:

- Any person who has parental responsibility for the child or
- With the leave of the court, the child her/himself

■ It is possible for an unmarried father who acquires parental responsibility by any of the following means to subsequently lose it:

- A Parental Responsibility Agreement or Parental Responsibility Order
- A Residence Order
- Appointment as a guardian either by a court or in the mother's will

NB. Re P [1995] 1FLR 1048 FD is to date, the only successful reported case on this point where parental responsibility was withdrawn from an unmarried father on an application by the child's mother consequent upon the child suffering injury at the hands of the father.

■ If acquired by means of an appointment as guardian, the court could in 'Family Proceedings' and on its own initiative terminate appointment as the child's guardian.

■ A father who acquires parental responsibility by jointly registering his child's birth with the mother can lose it **only** in the event of adoption or the child's death.

■ The court should expressly consider, in the case of an application by an unmarried father, the degree of commitment he has shown the child, degree of attachment which exists and reasons for the application [S. v. R. (Parental Responsibility) [1993] 1 FCR 331].

■ Tests of commitment, attachment and motivation are not exhaustive. Worrying injuries for which responsibility was not accepted justified refusal of the Order [Re H (Parental Responsibility) [1998] 1 FLR 855].

■ Denial of full contact [Re L (Contact: Trans-sexual Applicant) [1995] 2 FLR 438] or acrimony between parties [Re P (A Minor) (Parental Responsibility Order) [1994] 1 FLR 578] are not necessarily bars to a Parental Responsibility Order.

■ An example of a refusal to grant a Parental Responsibility Order because of violence and the applicant's refusal to comply with a court order for maintenance exists [Re T (A Minor) (Parental Responsibility: Contact) [1993] 1 FLR 450 CA].

Acquisition of Parental Responsibility by Step-Parent [s.4A inserted by s.112 ACA 2002]

■ s.4A has been amended by s.112 ACA 2002 to

provide that where a child's parent (parent A) who has parental responsibility for the child, is married to a person who is **not** the child's parent i.e. a step-parent:

- Parent A (or if the other parent also has parental responsibility, both parents) may by agreement with the step-parent provide for her/him to have parental responsibility for the child [s.4A(1)(a)] or
- The court may, on the application of the step-parent, order that s/he has parental responsibility for the child [s.4A(1)(b)]

■ An agreement under s.4A(1)(a) is a 'Parental Responsibility Agreement' and must satisfy s.4(2) i.e. it must be in the form prescribed by the Lord Chancellor [s.4A(2) inserted by s.112 ACA 2002].

■ A Parental Responsibility Agreement/Order under s.4A (1) (a) or (1) (b) respectively may only be brought to an end by an order of the court made on the application of any person who has parental responsibility, or with leave of the court the child her/himself [s.4A (3) (a)–(b)] and the court is satisfied that s/he has sufficient understanding to make the proposed application [s.4A (4)].

Effect of an Unmarried or a Step-Father Acquiring Parental Responsibility

■ The essence of parental responsibility is that it is a status not merely a set of rights, duties and powers

[Re S (Parental Responsibility) [1995] 2 FLR 648].

■ Nonetheless, the practical advantages of such a status would include a right/ability to:

- Receive educational reports and provide consent to school trips
- Consent to treatment for, and receive medical reports about the child
- Sign official papers e.g. passport application
- Prevent a mother removing child from the UK
- Object to a proposed change of name
- Object to child's accommodation by local authority and an ability to lawfully remove her/him
- Be regarded as a 'parent' for purposes of adoption proceedings

NB. So as to comply with Article 8(1) of the Convention, best practice is to treat the unmarried father who does not have parental responsibility as possessing full rights in, e.g. adoption proceedings [see the statement to this effect by Butler-Sloss P in Re B [2002] 1 FLR 365, which was not undermined by the House of Lords decision in the same case, reported [2002] 1 FLR 196.

Acquisition of Parental Responsibility by Other Individuals

■ An individual can also acquire parental responsibility if s/he:

- Is appointed as a child's guardian by a court or

in writing, e.g. a will, by a person who has parental responsibility

NB. This status takes effect only when both parents of a child are dead (unless the deceased parent had a Residence Order in her/his favour or was the only parent with parental responsibility [s.5 (7)]).

■ If a Residence Order is granted in favour of an individual s/he will gain and retain parental responsibility for as long as the Residence Order is in force [s.12(2)].

NB. A guardian has all the powers of a parent with parental responsibility. A non-parent with a Residence Order has a more limited form, e.g. s/he cannot consent to or refuse an application to free a child for adoption or adoption itself, nor appoint a guardian.

*A guardian appointed by a parent or guardian (**not** by a court) has a right to disclaim her/his appointment 'within a reasonable time of first knowing that the appointment has taken effect' [s.6 (5)].*

■ A non parent aged 18 or over can also acquire parental responsibility if an application to court is successful and a 'special guardianship order' is made in her/his favour.

Acquisition of Parental Responsibility by Local Authority

■ A local authority obtains parental responsibility if a court makes a child subject of a 'Care Order' [s.33 (3)].

■ A Care Order does not remove a parent's parental responsibility and allows the local authority to determine, where satisfied it is necessary to safeguard or promote child's welfare, the extent to which parent/guardian may continue to meet her/his parental responsibility.

   NB. A local authority with a Care Order cannot consent to or refuse an application to free a child for adoption, to adoption, appointment of a guardian or agree the child be brought up in a different religion [s.33(6)].

■ A local authority gains temporary parental responsibility if it obtains an Emergency Protection Order (EPO) [s.44 (4)] or an Interim Care Order [see Re B [2002] EWCA Civ 25 in the Times 29 January 2002].

■ Even with an EPO, the authority can only exercise its parental responsibility to the extent reasonably required to safeguard or promote the child's welfare [s.44 (5)].

Part II: Part II Orders

Part II Orders

s.8 Orders

- The following orders are available to all levels of courts in private applications and Care and Supervision proceedings, provided the court is also satisfied that making an order is better than making no order at all.

- With respect to a child 'in care' a court is empowered to grant only a Residence Order (as opposed to any of the other 3 s.8 orders) and this discharges the Care Order.

  *NB. No court may make **any** s.8 order to last beyond the child's 16th birthday **unless** it is satisfied that the circumstances of the case are exceptional [s.9 (6)]**or** s.12(5)(- Residence Orders – as inserted by the ACA 2002, applies – see below).*

Contact Order

■ A Contact Order directs a caregiver to allow a child contact with another person, by phone or in person.

NB. The Court of Appeal has determined a Contact Order can include an order requiring the caregiver not to allow the child contact with another person [Nottingham County Council v. P (No. 2) 1993].

■ The Advisory Board on Family Law (Children Act Sub-Committee) produced in 2000 'The Question of Parental Contact in Cases Where There Is Domestic Violence' and in 2002, 'Making Contact Work'. The former highlighted the importance of better recognition of domestic violence in contact applications and concluded practice guidelines from the Lord Chancellor and President of the Family Division were required.

■ Guidance was provided in Re L, V, M and H [2000] 2 FLR 334 to Magistrates and Judges by Dame Elizabeth Butler-Sloss (President of the High Court Family Division) in the Court of Appeal and stated that:

  • The court should take steps such as considering what evidence will be required if it believes proven allegations will affect its Contact Order
  • Court Welfare Officers (since re-named Children and Family Reporters and actually referred to as Family Court Advisers) should receive specific directions in cases involving domestic violence

- Magistrates and Judges should consider if the parent who has perpetrated domestic violence appreciates what the effect may have been on the child

NB. See also the reports of the Advisory Board on Family Law (Children Act Sub-Committee) 'Facilitation and Enforcement of Contact' [May 2002].

■ A Prohibited Steps Order is the more appropriate response if the court wishes to actively prevent a person making contact with a child [Re H (Prohibited Steps Order) (1995) 1 FLR 638].

Contact Activity Directions etc

■ The Children and Adoption Act 2006 (not in force at time of printing) inserts a s.11A-11G into the Children Act 1989.

■ Where the court is considering whether to make provision about contact by means of making or varying or discharging a Contact Order the above amendments introduce:

- 'Contact activity directions' (requiring an individual who is a party to proceedings to take part in an activity that promotes contact with the child concerned)
- Further provisions that describe the circumstances and conditions that must or may apply if contact directions are to be made
- The possibility of financial support for individuals required to take part in an activity

- The possibility of monitoring of the arrangements by a CAFCASS (or in Wales, Welsh Family Proceedings) officer

- S.11 H–N introduce:

  - Warning Notices
  - Enforcement Orders
  - Monitoring arrangements for these

NB. Subsequent editions of this guide will provide further details.

Prohibited Steps Order

■ A Prohibited Steps Order prevents someone from doing something which might ordinarily be done in fulfilling parental responsibility.

NB. Such an order must relate to an aspect of parental responsibility so (with some reservations) the House of Lords has determined that it could not include a ban on publicity [Re W (Wardship: Discharge: Publicity) [1995] 2 FLR 466].

The courts will have to bear in mind the provisions of Article 9 of the Convention (Right to Freedom of Thought, Conscience and Religion) when considering applications for Prohibited Steps or Specific Issue Orders [see decision in Re J (Circumcision) [2000] 1 FLR 571[CA].

Residence Order

■ A Residence Order settles with whom a child must live.

■ The order provides (for its duration) parental responsibility and cancels any existing Care Order [s.9].

■ The Court of Appeal had held that a 'Shared Residence Order' (child living for specified periods in different households) needed to be justified as having a positive benefit [A v A (Children's Shared Residence Order) [1994] 1 FLR 669] and was to be considered 'unusual' [Re H (Shared Residence: Parental Responsibility) [1995] 2 FLR 883].

■ More recently, in D v D (Shared Residence Order) (Court of Appeal; Dame Elizabeth Butler-Sloss P and Hale LJ [2001] 1 FLR 495 concluded that:

  • It was **not** necessary to demonstrate exceptional circumstances and that
  • So long as it could be shown to be in the child's best interests as per s.1, it might not even be necessary to demonstrate a positive benefit as such

■ In Re A (Children: Shared Residence) [2002] 1 FCR 177, the Court of Appeal whilst endorsing the view that shared Residence Orders were not necessarily to be regarded as exceptional, nevertheless emphasised such an order must reflect the real position on the ground.

- In the above case, the Court overturned an order which had been made in order to recognise the equal status of the parents, but where the boy was not only not living with his mother but was unlikely even to visit her.

- In a case where a child was born by artificial insemination by a donor into a lesbian relationship where both parties contributed significantly to care of the child but then separated, the non-parent was given leave under s.10 (9) to apply for a joint Residence Order on the basis it may be in the child's best interests for both adults to have parental responsibility [G v F (Contact and Shared Residence: Application for Leave [1998] 2 FLR 799].

- In the case of Re G [2005] 2 FLR 957 a case involving a same sex couple brought before the implementation of the CPA 2004, the Court of Appeal made an order for shared residence in favour of both partners, in order that the non-parent could continue to play a significant part in the life of the children whom she had brought up as her own. The Court of Appeal noted that the non-parent had been entitled to apply for a Residence Order under the provisions of s.10 (5) (b) CA 1989 as the children had lived with her and her partner for more than 3 years. Under the amendments effected to the CA 1989 by the CPA 2004, s10 (5) (aa), she would now be entitled to apply as of right, if she was a civil partner in a registered civil partnership.

- Courts can make a 'Joint Residence Order' (parties

living together) [Re C (A Minor) (Residence Order: Lesbian Co-Parents) [1994] Fam Law 468 and G v G [1993] Fam Law 615].

NB. In essence, there is a growing judicial readiness to contemplate shared care (for which a harmonious relationship between ex-partners is not a pre-requisite).

▪ It may very rarely be necessary to have an interim or 'without notice' Residence Order e.g. in a 'snatch situation' [Re G (Ex Parte Interim Residence Order) [1993] 1 FLR 910].

▪ In B v B (Residence Order: Restricting Applications) [1997] 139 CA, the Court of Appeal considered the correct criteria for deciding whether to prohibit future applications without leave of the court pursuant to s.91(14) of the Act. The court determined that such an order was a Draconian one and should **only** be used:

- 'Where a party...goes on making applications which are unrealistic, inappropriate, unlikely to have any chance of success because that parent is unable to see that litigation must stop...' and/or
- 'Where a party...has crossed the line from making applications which it is his right to make, to making applications which are...oppressive, or...vexatious...and/or
- 'Whether the best interests of the child require interference with the fundamental freedom of a

parent to raise issues affecting the child's welfare before a court as and when such issues arise.'

NB. These criteria apply to s.91 (14) applications for any orders under the Children Act 1989.

The use of s.91 (14) orders may be challenged as being in breach of Article 6 of the Convention (Right To a Fair Trial).

■ Re P (A Child) (Residence Order: Restriction Order) [1999] 3 All ER, concerned a non-practising Catholic family who, following 6 years of devoted care of a now 8 year old girl with Down's syndrome gained a Residence Order (the local authority having failed to recruit a suitable Jewish family).

■ The birth family applied for a variation of the order contending a child had a presumptive right to be brought up by her/his own parents and in her/his own religion.

■ The court held that the Children Act 1989 contained no presumption which could displace the welfare of the child as the paramount consideration.

■ The child's religious and cultural heritage was a relevant factor in considering her welfare, but only one to be weighed in the balance and not in this case an overwhelming one.

■ The power of a court to make a Residence Order in favour of any person who is not the parent or guardian of the child concerned, includes a power to direct, at the request of that person, that the order continues until the child is 18 (unless ended earlier) and any power to vary a Residence Order is exercisable accordingly [s.12 (5) inserted by s.114 ACA 2002].

Specific Issue Order

■ A Specific Issue Order resolves a particular problem e.g. education/medical treatment, or change of name.

■ In Re A [2000] 1 FLR 121, the court granted a Specific Issue Order providing that children of a French father and English mother should attend a Lycee in London whilst living with their mother in order to reflect their part French parentage.

■ Leave of a court to change a child's surname is required if a Residence Order is in force [s.13 (1)] or there is disagreement between 2 or more people who have parental responsibility.

■ Otherwise issues as to names should be dealt with as a Specific Issue Order sought by either parent as required [Re PC (Change of Surname) [1997] 2 FLR 730].

■ In the case of Re R (Surname: Using Both Parents') [2001] 2 FLR 1358 the Court dealing with a Spanish mother, ordered the use of both the mother's and father's surname as was the custom in Spain.

■ The House of Lords has confirmed that when an application is made to change a child's surname the court has to apply the criteria in s.1 and should not make the order unless there is evidence that it would lead to an improvement in the child's welfare.

■ Registration of the name is a relevant, important

factor but not 'all important' and does not render irrelevant well recognised considerations which weigh in favour of a child having the same surname as her/his natural father [Dawson v Wearmouth [1999[1 FLR 1167).

■ A change of forename as oppose to surname is also a very significant matter to be treated with appropriate seriousness e.g. no foster parent or carer should unilaterally change it [Re D, L and LA (Care: Change of Forename) [2003] 1 FLR 339 FD].

NB. In Re J (Specific Issue Orders: Child's Religious Upbringing and Circumcision) 2000 1 FLR, Thorpe LJ and Dame Butler Sloss P in the Court of Appeal agreed there was a small group of important or exceptional decisions which ought not to be taken without the consent of others who have parental responsibility or a court. Case law suggests these include change of surname, medical interventions e.g. circumcision or sterilisation and immunisation against infectious diseases [see Re C [2003] 2FLR 1095] changes of surname [see Re S [2001] 2 FLR 1005] or change of school or type of education [see Re P [2003]1 FLR 286, in which the Court of Appeal emphasised that the courts must not abdicate from their duty to decide such matters where the parents cannot agree.

Arguments could also be made based on Article 8(1) that the father's and/or his child's right to respect to family life has been breached by change of the children's surname.

Preference for Residence/ Contact Order [s.9]

■ A court will not grant a Specific Issue or Prohibited Steps Order if a Residence or Contact Order could achieve the same result.

Automatic Entitlement to Apply for Any s.8 Order [s.10 (4) as amended by Sch.3 para.56 ACA 2002]

■ A parent, guardian, special guardian, step parent (which includes a civil partner step parent) who has acquired parental responsibility via s.4A, or a Residence Order holder is entitled to apply for any s.8 order.

NB. The Court of Appeal has confirmed that 'parent' in this context includes an unmarried father [M. v. C. and Calderdale MBC 1992].

Automatic Entitlement to Apply for Residence or Contact Order [s.10 (5)]

■ The following have automatic entitlement to apply for a Residence or Contact Order, or for variation or discharge thereof:

- Any party to a marriage where a child is 'a child of the family' e.g. a stepchild
- Any civil partner in a civil partnership in relation to whom the child is a child of the family
- Anyone with whom the child had been living for a period of 3 years which need not have been continuous but which must have begun not

more than 5 years before the making of the application.
- Where a Residence Order exists, anyone with the consent of all holders
- Anyone with the consent of all who hold parental responsibility (if child is 'in care', this includes the local authority as well as the parents)

Automatic Entitlement to Apply for a Residence Order [s.10 (5A)]

■ A local authority foster carer is entitled to apply for a Residence Order if the child has lived with her/him for a period of 1 year immediately preceding the application [s.10(5A) introduced by the ACA 2002].

Entitlement to Seek Court's Leave to Make Application for Any s.8 Order [ss.9 &10 as amended by s.113 & Sch.3 para.56 ACA 2002]

■ The following are entitled to seek the court's leave to make an application for any s.8 Order:

- A child if the court is satisfied s/he has sufficient understanding
- A local authority foster carer if s/he was the foster carer within the last 6 months and has the local authority's consent, is a relative or is eligible because the child has lived with her/him for at least 1 year preceding the application
- Anyone else once the court has considered the criteria set out in s.10 (9)

■ The local authority cannot apply for Residence or Contact Order nor may these orders be made in its favour, though it could apply for a Prohibited Steps or Specific Issue Order for a child being cared for by a parent/other care giver or being 'accommodated'.

■ A court can, in Family Proceedings, make a s.8 Order even if no application has been received [s.10 (1) (b)].

■ Applications by a child are considered to raise issues more appropriate for determination by the High Court and should be transferred there for hearing according to the direction of the then President of High Court Family Division in February 1993.

■ It has been suggested that this direction is in breach of Article 6 (Right to a Fair Trial) and the 'Equality of Arms' principle used by the European Court in such cases.

■ In Re A (Contact: Separate Representation) [2001] 1 FLR 715, Dame Elizabeth Butler-Sloss P, Potter and Hale JJ granted leave to appeal against a County Court judgement that a 4 year old girl whose mother has sought separate representation on the child's behalf by the National Youth Advocacy Service (NYAS)) should not be granted it. The Court of Appeal ordered that the child should be represented by the Official Solicitor not NYAS and supported the argument that the decision in the County Court risked there being a breach of this girl's rights under Articles 3, 6, and 8 of the European Convention.

- It has also been suggested that provision of s.10 (8) restricting children's participation in s.8 proceedings to those cases in which they seek to be made a party is also in breach generally of children's rights to representation, protected by Articles 6, 8 and 14 of the Convention and also a breach of Article 12 UNCRC (see the very important Court of Appeal decision in Mabon v Mabon [2005] 2 FLR 1011).

NB. Amendments to s.93 (2) and s.41 (6) (a) introduced by the ACA 2002 provide for the Lord Chancellor to designate s.8 proceedings as 'specified proceedings' under s.41 CA 1989 and thus allow for orders to be made for the separate representation of children in such proceedings. It should be noted that the Lord Chancellor has still not so provided, and thus children in such proceedings are not entitled to separate representation as of right.

Criteria for Granting Leave to Make a s.8 Application [s.10 (9)]

- The court must in deciding whether or not to grant leave, have particular regard to:

  - The nature of the proposed application
  - The applicant's connection with the child
  - Any risk there might be of the proposed application disrupting the child's life to such an extent s/he would be harmed by it, and
  - (Where a child is being looked after by a local authority), its plans for her/his future and wishes/feelings of her/his parents

NB. For purposes of seeking leave to make an application, the child's welfare is not the paramount consideration (because s.1 (1) does not apply). Except in an emergency, the interests of justice require notice of application for leave to be given to all parties likely to be affected (see Re M (Prohibited Steps Order: Application for Leave) 1993 1 FLR 275 and Re W (A Child: Contact Leave To Apply) 2000 1 FLR 185].

Application for Variation or Discharge of s.8 Order [s.10]

■ The following are entitled to apply for variation or discharge of a s.8 order:

- Anyone entitled to apply for a s.8 order or who has the leave of the court
- Any civil partner in a civil partnership in relation to whom the child is a child of the family
- A parent, guardian, special guardian or any holder of a Residence Order
- A person who has parental responsibility by virtue of s.4A

■ The following persons may apply for a variation/discharge of a Residence or Contact Order:

- Any party to a marriage (whether or not subsisting) where child is a 'child of the family'
- Any civil partner in a civil partnership in relation to whom the child is a child of the family
- Any person with whom child has lived for total

of 3 years in period 3 months to 5 years prior to application

- A local authority foster carer if the child has lived with her/him for at least 1 year preceding the application
- Where a Residence Order is in force, any person with consent of each person in whose favour the Residence Order exists
- If child in local authority care, any person with the consent of the local authority, or
- In any other case, with the consent of those (if any) with parental responsibility
- Anyone on whose application a s.8 order was previously made
- A person named in a Contact Order
- Any person prescribed by rules of court

Appeals [s.94]

- To Family Division of High Court against a magistrates' court decision to make/refuse to make a s.8 Order.

- To Court of Appeal Civil Division against making/refusal to make such orders by a Judge in County or High Court.

Special Guardianship [s.14A–G introduced by s.115 ACA 2002]

Purpose of Special Guardianship Orders

- Special Guardianship Orders are intended to meet the needs of children who cannot live with their birth parents, for whom adoption is not appropriate but who could still benefit from a legally secure placement.

- These conditions were found to be met in the case of A Local Authority v Y, Z and Others [2006] Fam Law 448, which is thought to be the first ever reported case on the making of Special Guardianship Orders.

- In this case, the court determined special guardianship was the most appropriate order where 2 older children from a family of 5 had been placed by the local authority with an aunt and uncle for 2 years and the 3rd child had been placed with another aunt and her partner for almost 2 years. The youngest 2 children had been placed for adoption. The Court emphasised special guardianship would serve the best interests of the 3 older children: it was in accordance with their wishes; they had been with the particular couples for 2 years; had made progress during that time; and the relationships needed cementing. The children (said the Court), required the permanence stability and security that special guardianship would provide; it was preferable to alternatives under the CA 1989; and adoption was neither sought nor desirable.

■ The court also made an order for defined contact with the mother. This case recognises the intended half-way house outcome of special guardianship in that it confers security for the child in that the Special Guardians have parental responsibility yet preserves the parent/child relationship and it can, if required, be varied or discharged.

Definition & Conditions for Making a Special Guardianship Order [s.14A]

■ A Special Guardianship Order is an order appointing 1 or more individuals to be 'special guardian/s' for a child [s.14A (1)].

■ A special guardian must:

  • Be aged 18 or over and
  • Not be a parent of the child in question [s.14A(2)]

■ The court may make a Special Guardianship Order with respect to any child on the application of an individual (or joint application of more than 1 such individual – couples need not be married) who:

  • Is/are entitled to make such an application with respect to the child or
  • Has/have obtained the leave of the court to make the application [s.14A(3)]

NB. A person who is, or was at any time within the last 6 months, a local authority foster carer of a child may not apply for a Special Guardianship Order with *respect to that child **unless** s/he has the authority's consent, is a relative or the child has lived with her/him for a total of at least 1 year preceding the application [effect of s.14A (4)].*

Eligibility to Make an Application for Special Guardianship Order [s.14A (5)–(7)]

■ The individuals who are entitled to apply for a Special Guardianship Order with respect to a child are:

- Any guardian of the child
- Any individual in whose favour a residence order is in force with respect to the child
- Any person with whom the child has lived for at least 3 years (in the period 3 months to 5 years before the application is made)
- Where a Residence Order is in force with respect to the child, any person who has consent of those in whose favour the Residence Order was made
- Where the child is in the care of the local authority, any person who has the consent of that authority
- Any person who has the consent of each of those (if any) who have parental responsibility
- A local authority foster carer with whom the child has lived for a period of at least 1 year immediately preceding the application [s.14A(5)]

■ The court may also make a Special Guardianship Order with respect to a child in any family proceedings in which a question arises with respect to the welfare of the child if:

- An application for the order has been made by an individual (or more than 1 such individual jointly) who is entitled to or has obtained the court's leave
- The court considers that a Special Guardianship Order should be made even though no such application has been made [s.14A(6)]

■ No individual may make an application under s.14A (3) or (6) unless, s/he has given 3 months written notice of her/his intention to make the application:

- (If the child in question is being looked after by a local authority), to that local authority, or
- Otherwise, to the local authority in whose area the individual is ordinarily resident [s.14A(7)]

Response to Application for Special Guardianship Order [s.14A (8)–(13)]

■ On receipt of such a notice, the local authority must investigate the matter and prepare a report for the court.

■ The court may itself ask a local authority to conduct such an investigation and prepare a report, and the local authority is obliged to do so [s.14A (8); (9)].

NB. The local authority may make such arrangements as it sees fit for any person to act on its behalf in connection with conducting the investigation or preparing the report [s.14A (10)].

■ The court may not make a Special Guardianship Order unless it has received a report dealing with the matters referred to in s.14A (8) [s.14A (11)].

■ Where a person applies for leave to make an application for a Special Guardianship Order, the court in deciding whether to grant leave must have particular regard to:

- The nature of the proposed application
- The applicant's connection with the child
- Any risk there might be of that proposed application disrupting the child's life to such an extent that s/he would be harmed by it and
- (Where s/he is looked after by a local authority) the authority's plans for her/his future and the wishes and feelings of the parents [s.14A (12)]

*NB. When a Placement Order is in force, no Special Guardianship Order may be made in respect of a child **unless** an application has been made for an Adoption Order and the applicant for the Special Guardianship Order has obtained the court's leave under s.29 (5) **or** (if s/he is a guardian of the child) has obtained the court's leave under s.47 (5). Where leave has been given, the requirement for 3 months notice in s.14A (7) applications does not apply [effect of s.14A (13)].*

Making a Special Guardianship Order [s.14B]

■ Before making a Special Guardianship Order, the court must consider whether, if the order were made:

- A Contact Order should also be made with respect

NB. This was done in the case of A Local Authority v Y,Z and Others [2006] Fam Law 448,where an order for defined contact was made in favour of the mother(see above)

- Any s.8 order in force with respect to the child should be varied or discharged [s.14B(1)]

■ On making a Special Guardianship Order, the court may also:

- Give leave for the child to be known by a new surname
- Grant the leave required by s.14C(3)(b), either generally or for specified purposes [s.14B(2)]

Effect of a Special Guardianship Order [s.14C]

■ The effect of a Special Guardianship Order is that while the order remains in force:

- A special guardian appointed by the order has parental responsibility for the child and
- Subject to any other order in force with respect to the child under the Children Act, is entitled to exercise parental responsibility to the exclusion of any other person with parental responsibility for the child (apart from another special guardian) [s.14C(1)]

■ A special guardian is **not** entitled to provide consent to key decisions where statute or case law require the consent of more than 1 person with parental responsibility in a matter affecting the child e.g:

- Sterilisation/circumcision
- Adoption or placement for adoption

■ While a Special Guardianship Order is in force with respect to a child, no person may (without either the written consent of every person who has parental responsibility for the child or leave of the court):

- Cause the child to be known by a new surname or
- Remove her/him from the UK [s.14C(3)]

*NB. The child's special guardian **is** allowed to remove the child from the UK for a period of less than 3 months, [s.14C (4)].*

■ If the child with respect to whom a Special Guardianship Order is in force dies, her/his special guardian must take reasonable steps to give notice of that fact to each:

- Parent of the child with parental responsibility and
- Guardian of the child

NB. If the child has more than 1 special guardian, and 1 has taken such steps in relation to a particular parent or guardian, any other special guardian need not also do so [s.14C (5)].

Variation and Discharge of a Special Guardianship Order [s.14D]

■ The court may vary or discharge a Special Guardianship Order on the application of:

- The special guardian (or any of them, if there is more than 1)
- Any parent or guardian of the child concerned
- Any individual in whose favour a Residence Order is in force with respect to the child
- Any individual not falling into the above categories, who has, or immediately before the making of the special guardianship order had, parental responsibility for the child
- The child her/himself or
- A local authority designated in a Care Order with respect to the child [s.14D(1)]

■ In any family proceedings in which a question arises with respect to the welfare of a child with respect to whom a Special Guardianship Order is in force, the court may also vary or discharge that order if it considers that it should be varied or discharged, even though no application has been made under s.14D (1) [s.14D (2)].

■ The following must obtain the leave of the court before making an application under s.14D(1):

- The child
- Any parent or guardian of her/him
- Any step-parent who has acquired, and has not lost, parental responsibility for by virtue of s.4A

- Any individual (other than special guardian, parent or guardian or in whose favour a Residence Order is on force) who immediately before the making of the Special Guardianship Order had, but no longer has, parental responsibility for her/him

■ Where the person applying for leave to make an application under s.14D(1) is the child, the court may only grant leave if it is satisfied that s/he has sufficient understanding to make the proposed application [s.14D(4)].

■ The court may not grant leave to a person (other than the child) under s.14D (3) unless it is satisfied that there has been a significant change in circumstances since the making of the Special Guardianship Order [s.14D (5)].

Special Guardianship Order: Supplementary Provisions [s.14E]

■ In proceedings in which any question of making, varying or discharging a Special Guardianship Order arises, the court must (in the light of any rules made by virtue of 14E(3):

- Draw up a timetable with a view to determining the question without delay and
- Give such directions as it considers appropriate for the purpose of ensuring, so far as is reasonably practicable, that the timetable is adhered to [s.14E(1)]

NB. S.14E (1) applies also in relation to proceedings in which any other question with respect to a Special Guardianship Order arises. A Special Guardianship Order, or an order varying one, may contain provisions which are to have effect for a specified period [s.14E (4)].

Special Guardianship Order Support Services [14F]

■ Each local authority must make arrangements for the provision within its area of special guardianship support services i.e:

- Counselling, advice and information and
- Such other services as are prescribed [s.14F(1)]

■ At the request of any of the following persons, a local authority may carry out an assessment of that person's needs for special guardianship support services:

- A child with respect to whom a Special Guardianship Order is in force
- A special guardian
- A parent

■ A local authority may, at the request of any other person, carry out an assessment of that person's needs for special guardianship support services [s.14F (4)].

■ Where, as a result of an assessment, a local authority decides that a person has needs for special guardianship support services, it must then decide whether to provide any such services to that person [s.14F(5)]

- The local authority must prepare a plan in accordance with which special guardianship support services are to be provided to the person and keep the plan under review, **if** the:

  - Local authority decides to provide any special guardianship support services to a person, and
  - Circumstances fall within a prescribed description [s.14F(6) Children Act 1989]

- A local authority may provide special guardianship support services (or any part of them) by securing their provision by:

  - Another local authority; or
  - A person as defined in the Special Guardianship Support Services Regulations 2005

  NB. A local authority may also arrange with any such authority or person for that other authority or that person to carry out the local authority's functions in relation to assessments under s.14.

- A local authority may carry out an assessment of the needs of any person for the purposes of special guardianship at the same time as an assessment of her/his needs is made under any other provision of the Children Act or under any other enactment [s.14F(10) Children Act 1989]

- S.27 (co-operation between authorities) applies in relation to the exercise of functions of a local authority introduced by s.115 as it applies in relation to the exercise of functions of a local authority under Part 3 [s.14F(11) Children Act 1989].

Special Guardianship Order Support Services: Representations [14G Children Act 1989]

■ Every local authority is obliged to establish a procedure for considering representations (including complaints) made to it by any person to whom it may provide special guardianship support services about the discharge of its functions under s.14 F (1) in relation to her/him [s.14G(1) Children Act 1989 inserted by ACA 2002].

■ The Children Act 1989 Representations Procedure (England) Regulations 2006 Regulations have been made by the Secretary of State pursuant to s.14G (2) Children Act 1989 (inserted by ACA 2002), providing for such procedures to be in place in relation to any functions associated with the provision of special guardianship support services (see reg. 5) and imposing under reg. 9(1) a time limit of 1 year on the making of the above representations.

■ The Regulations go on to provide that a local authority **may** consider any representations outside the time limit if, having regard to all the circumstances, it concludes that it would not be reasonable to expect the complainant to have made the representations within the time limit (reg. 9(2)(a); and notwithstanding the time that has passed it is still possible to consider the representations effectively and fairly (reg.(2)(b).

Family Assistance Orders (F.A.O) [s.16 as amended by Sch.3 para.56 ACA 2002 & s.6 CAA 2006]

■ In those family proceedings in which a court is able to grant s.8 orders, including Care, Supervision and Education Supervision Orders, it is also able to grant, on its own or in combination with a s.8 Order, an F.A.O.

■ A F.A.O. is granted only in exceptional circumstances e.g. Re E (Family Assistance Order) [1999] 2 FLR 512 when an F.A.O. was made against a new local authority into whose area the child had moved to maintain vital contact with a mother detained in a psychiatric unit for murdering the child's father.

■ A F.A.O. requires the consent of all those named in it (other than the child) and obliges the supervisor (usually a CAFCASS officer or possibly a local authority social worker) to advise, assist and befriend child/parent/guardian/special guardian/caregiver/holder of Contact Order.

■ A F.A.O. lasts 6 months unless the court specifies a shorter period.

■ A F.A.O. cannot be made requiring a local authority to make an officer available unless the local authority agrees or the child lives within its area.

NB. However, in Re C (Family Assistance Order)

*1996 3 FCR 514, in which a Director of Social
Services was reluctant to allocate an officer though
the child did live within the area, Johnson J
considered it would not be appropriate to attach a
penal notice to the F.A.O.*

■ S.6 CAA 2006 (not in force at the time of
publication) amends s.16 and:

- Removes the need (s.16(3)(a) for the
  circumstances to be 'exceptional'
- Inserts a new subsection 4A of section 16so that
  if the court makes a F.A.O to be in force at the
  same time as a Contact Order, it may direct the
  officer concerned give advice/assistance about
  establishing, improving and maintaining contact
- Increases the maximum duration of a F.A.O to 12
  months

Part III: Support for Children & Families

Determination of 'Need' – Children Act 1989 [s.17 (10)]

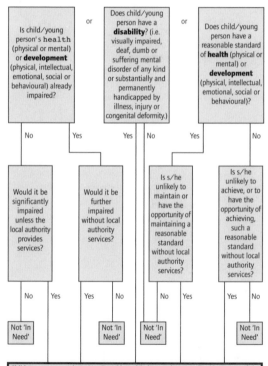

Is child/young person's **health** (physical or mental) or **development** (physical, intellectual, emotional, social or behavioural) already impaired?

or

Does child/young person have a **disability**? (i.e. visually impaired, deaf, dumb or suffering mental disorder of any kind or substantially and permanently handicapped by illness, injury or congenital deformity.)

or

Does child/young person have a reasonable standard of **health** (physical or mental) or **development** (physical, intellectual, emotional, social or behavioural)?

No — Yes

Yes — No

Yes — No

Would it be significantly impaired unless the local authority provides services?

Would it be further impaired without local authority services?

Is s/he unlikely to maintain or have the opportunity of maintaining a reasonable standard without local authority services?

Is s/he unlikely to achieve, or to have the opportunity of achieving, such a reasonable standard without local authority services?

No — Yes

Yes — No

No — Yes

Yes — No

Not 'In Need'

Not 'In Need'

Not 'In Need'

Not 'In Need'

Child/young person is 'In Need' and is entitled to services described in Part III of the Children Act 1989. If necessary, services should be delivered via those with parental responsibility or with whom the child has been living.

Support for Children & Families

General Duty [s.17 (1)]

■ Each local authority has a general duty to safeguard and promote welfare of children 'in need' within its area and, insofar as is consistent with that duty, to promote their upbringing by their families by providing a range and level of services appropriate to their needs.

■ For an interpretation of 'within its area', see A v Lambeth CC [2001] 2 FLR 1201 applied also in R on the application of Stewart v Wandsworth London Borough Council [2001] All ER D 8 October 200.

■ In the above case/s, a mother applied for support in respect of children where she lived in Lambeth, in a hostel owned by Hammersmith whilst her children went to school in Wandsworth. It was held that both Lambeth and Wandsworth owed duties to the children.

Definition of Need [s.17 (10); (11)]

■ A child is 'in need' if:

  • S/he is unlikely to achieve or maintain, or have opportunity to so do, a reasonable standard of health or development without provision of services by a local authority, or if her/his

  • Health or development is likely to be significantly impaired, or further impaired, without such services, or

- S/he is disabled

NB. Health = physical or mental; Development = physical, intellectual, emotional, social or behavioural; Disabled = blind, deaf, dumb or suffering from mental disorder of any kind or substantially and permanently handicapped by illness, injury or congenital deformity, or other such disability as may be prescribed.

Providing Accommodation for Children in Need [s.17 as amended by s.116 ACA 2002]

■ Services provided in the exercise of a local authority's duties under s.17 (6) may include providing accommodation, giving assistance in kind or, in exceptional circumstances, in cash.

*NB. Those provided with accommodation under s.17 are **not** 'looked after, so for purposes of s.22 (1) (b) as amended by s.116 ACA 2002 (general duties toward looked after children, s.22 duties do **not** apply.*

Inter Agency Co-operation [s.27]

■ A mutual obligation exists for local authorities to assist one another unless this is in conflict with their own statutory duties (see R on application of Stewart v Wandsworth cited above).

Day Care [s.18]

■ A local authority must provide such day care for preschool children aged 5 and under 'in need' and care and supervised activities for school children 'in need' within its area outside school hours and in holidays as is appropriate.

NB. The meaning of 'appropriate' was considered in the case of R v London Borough of Brent ex parte B 1994 1 FLR 592.

■ In so doing the local authority must have regard to racial groups to which such children belong [Sch.2 para.11].

■ The Children Act 2004 revoked previous duties to produce a number of plans including the 'early years' development and child care partnership plan' and introduced an obligation to produce a triennial strategic 'children and young people's' plan to be updated annually[s.17 Children Act 2004].

NB. The Childcare Act 2006 (not in force at the time of printing) will place substantial new duties on local authorities to improve outcomes for young children by means of securing sufficient childcare and providing information to parents. CAE plans to produce a guide to this new legislation in early 2007.

Domiciliary Support [Sch.2 para.8]

■ The local authority is empowered to provide advice, guidance, counselling; occupational, social, cultural or recreational activities; home helps (including laundry facilities) and travel subsidies to access other support services and assistance with holidays.

Direct Payments & Vouchers [s.17A & 17B introduced by s.7 Carers and Disabled Children Act 2000]

- Instead of itself providing the services which s.17 allows, the local authority may make direct payments to enable the purchase of required service/s for those aged less than 18 and who have a disability, to:

  - Those who have parental responsibility for the child or
  - Directly to a young person aged 16 or 17

  NB. Vouchers expressed in terms of time, money or period of short-break services may also be issued to a person with parental responsibility.

Reduction of Need for Care Proceedings etc. [Sch.2 para.7]

- The local authority must take reasonable steps to:

  - Reduce care/criminal/family proceedings leading to care
  - Avoid need for secure accommodation
  - Encourage children not to commit crime

Prevention of Neglect & Abuse [Sch.2 para.4]

- The local authority must take reasonable steps through provision of family support services to prevent children within its area suffering ill treatment or neglect.

■ The local authority must inform any other local authority if a child likely to suffer harm lives, or proposes to live in its area.

Accommodation to Protect Child [Sch. 2 para.5]

■ If it appears to it, that a child living on particular premises is suffering or is likely to suffer ill treatment at the hands of another person living there, and that other person proposes to move out, the local authority may assist her/him to obtain alternative accommodation.

Family Centres [Sch.2 para.9]

■ The local authority may also provide in family centres, advice, counselling, recreational activities etc. and accommodation for children, parents, those with parental responsibility and those with whom child is living.

General Duty to Accommodate [s.20 (1)]

■ The local authority must provide accommodation for a child for whom nobody has parental responsibility or who is lost or when, for any reason, the ordinary caregiver is prevented from providing suitable accommodation or care.

Duty to Accommodate Certain Young People Aged 16–17 inc. [s.20 (3)]

■ The local authority must provide accommodation to

children 'in need' in this age group if their welfare would otherwise be 'seriously prejudiced'.

NB. This duty may be enforceable [Re T (Accommodation by Local Authority) [1995] 1 FLR 159].

Power To Accommodate Young Persons 16–20 years inc. [s.20 (5)]

■ A local authority may provide accommodation in any community home which accepts those 16 or over, if it considers it would safeguard or promote the young person's welfare.

Removal from Accommodation [s.20 (7)] as amended by Sch.3 para.59 ACA 2002]

■ Anyone with parental responsibility may remove a child unless s/he is 16 or 17 and disagrees.

■ Effective agreements with parents should reduce potential problems but if 'significant harm' appears likely, emergency protection measures are available.

NB. A holder of a Residence Order or a special guardian can authorise retention of a child in accommodation in spite of a parent's wishes to remove her/him.

Other Obligations to Accommodate [s.21]

■ When asked, a local authority must accommodate a child:

- Removed from home on an Emergency Protection or Child Assessment Order
- Subject of Police Powers of Protection
- Remanded (allows detention of child)
- Detained under Police & Criminal Evidence Act 1984
- On a 'Supervision Order' with residence requirements (Children & Young Persons Act 1969 [s.12 AA])

Local Authority Duties toward Looked After Children [ss.22; 23; Sch.2 para.15, & 19A]

■ Safeguard and promote welfare and make reasonable efforts to allow child access to ordinary services as though still at home [s.22 (3)].

NB. Potentially, the above is a very onerous duty of care owed both to safeguard and promote the child's welfare. There also exists the common law duty of care owed by the local authority to children being looked after under a care order or those who are being accommodated by the local authority.

Even before the decision in Z v UK [2001] 2 FLR 612 (the old X v Bedfordshire CC [1995] 2 FLR 276 case when heard in the English Courts), it had been determined in Barrett v London Borough Council of Enfield [1999] 2 FLR 426 that the local authority owed a common law duty of care towards children in its care. See also for the duty of care in respect of particular decisions taken by individual social workers W v Essex County Council [2000] 1 FLR 657, where the Court of Appeal had held by a majority that a local authority may be liable in negligence and in negligent mis-statement in relation to specific statements made on its behalf by a social worker to prospective foster parents. The foster parents in W alleged that a teenager had been placed with them contrary to specific reassurances given to them by the social worker that no adolescent known or suspected to be a child sexual abuser would be fostered with them. The teenager who was placed with them had in fact been cautioned for indecent assault, which was known to the local authority social worker and then after placement went on to sexually abuse the foster parent's 4 children who then suffered psychiatric illnesses as a result of the trauma. In this case, which was decided before Z (see above) the majority of the Court of Appeal held that the case was distinguishable from X v Bedfordshire County Council in that this case involved harm caused by a child in care to the family in which he was placed. The Court of Appeal, however, did not allow the parents' case to proceed. The appeal to the House of Lords by the parents was allowed and the House reversed the decision, in that they allowed the parents as well as the children, to lodge their claim that they had also suffered as a result of the actions of Social Services.

See also the decision in F v Lambeth London Borough Council [2002] 1 FLR 217 where in this case 2 boys suffered serious harm whilst in the care of the local authority, which had failed to place them with foster parents and had also failed to facilitate contact between the boys and their family. Thus the local authority was held liable in damages for breach of duty of care and for breach of particular sections of the CA 1989 e.g. s22(3), (4),and (5) and s23(7),with Munby J. taking the unusual step of giving judgement in open court so that the failures of the local authority could be noted by the Press.

And see C v Flintshire County Council [2001] 2 FLR 33 where a girl, who had been the subject of a care order due to parental abuse, was seriously bullied and abused whilst in care, and again recovered damages for injuries sustained as a result of the breach of the duty of care.

See also A and B v Essex County Council [2003] 1 FLR 615 where Munby J held that where social workers from Essex Social Services had failed to pass on information about a boy's serious behavioural difficulties (which included being very violent towards his sister who had been placed with the same prospective adoptive parents) to the prospective adoptive parents, then the social workers had failed in their common law duty of care in that they had not provided all the relevant information about the children to A and B and so Essex CC was vicariously liable for any breaches of care established. However, once the prospective adoptive parents continued with the placement after they were fully aware of all the circumstances then at that point the authority's negligence had run its course and no further liability for subsequent problems could arise. Damage sustained after the adoption was not therefore caused by the authority's breach of duty.

■ Endeavour, unless not reasonably practical or consistent with welfare, to promote contact between child and

- Parents, and anyone else who has parental responsibility. This duty on the local authority to promote contact was found to have been

breached in F v Lambeth London Borough
Council [2002] 1 FLR 217 (see above).
- Relatives, friends or persons connected with
  her/him

■ Take reasonable steps to keep parents and those
who hold parental responsibility informed of child's
location.

■ Not to place a child with a disability in unsuitable
accommodation.

■ Consult child (according to age and understanding),
parent/s, those with parental responsibility and
other 'relevant' people [s.22 (4); (5) – found to have
been breached in F v Lambeth London Borough
Council [2002] 1 FLR 217 (see above)].

*NB. In deciding to remove a child from a foster carer,
the local authority must consult her/him as well as
any children's guardian who has been involved [R v
Hereford and Worcester County Council ex parte D
[1992] 1 FLR 448].*

■ Before making any decision, consider child's race,
culture, religion and linguistic background.

*NB. The local authority may act contrary to the above
in order to protect the public from serious injury.*

■ So far as is practicable and consistent with welfare,
place a child with parents, or someone with parental
responsibility (for a child 'in care' with any previous
Residence Order holder), relatives or friends [s.23
(6)] or other person connected with child.

NB. Failure to consider, consult and record compliance with such duties will give rise to allegations of a breach of Article 8(1) of the Convention. Thus in **Re M [2001] 2 FLR 1300** *the local authority had failed to involve the parents in a permanency planning meeting being held on in respect of their child T who had originally been made the subject of a Care Order as a result of failings in both parents who had a history of drug and alcohol abuse. Whilst still on the Care Order T had returned to live with her mother but then had to be removed from her care when the mother was taken into hospital following drug and alcohol poisoning. Shortly after this the local authority decided to and held a meeting to discuss T's future care, including potential adoption if placement with the maternal grandmother did not prove viable. Because of various problems they failed to invite either the parents or their solicitors with whom the local authority had been in contact. Holman J held that the local authority had been in breach of the requirements of Article 8 ECHR taken together with s.6 HRA 1998. Thus the decision of the planning meeting was unlawful and would be quashed. Further, the very fundamental change of plan being put forward by the local authority also breached the parents' rights under Art 8 and the Court ordered that everything should be reviewed at a later full hearing in court where the court would determine what should happen and would also deal with specific applications for the discharge of the Care Order.*

■ If child must be placed with strangers, ensure s/he is near home and with any siblings [s.23 (7) found to have been breached in F v Lambeth London Borough Council [2002] 1 FLR 217 (see above).]

■ Advise, assist and befriend the child with a view to promoting her/his welfare when s/he ceases to be looked after [Sch.2 para.19A introduced by s.1 Children (Leaving Care) Act 2000].

Review Duties [s.26 as amended by s.118 ACA 2002]

■ Each local authority, for a child in its care must:

• Keep her/his s.31A plan under review and if it is of the opinion that some change is required, to revise it and make a new plan

• Consider whether an application should be made to discharge the Care Order found to have been breached in F v Lambeth London Borough Council [2002] 1 FLR 217 (see above)

■ A local authority which is 'providing accommodation' for a child i.e. one who is not subject of a Care Order, must:

• If there is no plan for her/his future, prepare one

• If there is such a plan, keep it under review and if of the opinion that some change is required, to revise the plan or make a new one – found to have been breached in F v Lambeth London Borough Council [2002] 1 FLR 217 (see above)

- The Review of Children's Cases (Amendment) (England) Regulations 2004 require each responsible authority to appoint an independent reviewing officer (IRO) for each case to carry out the functions of s.26(2A), i.e. to:

  - Participate in reviews of the case in question
  - Monitor the performance of the authority in respect of the reviews and
  - Refer the case to an officer of CAFCASS if s/he considers it appropriate to do so

- The IRO must be a registered social worker and have sufficient social work experience to undertake the functions required of her/him. An employee of the responsible authority must not be appointed as an IRO if s/he is involved in management of the case or is under the management of a person:

  - Involved in management of the case
  - With management responsibilities for the above person or
  - With control over resources allocated to the case

NB. The IRO must as far as is reasonably practicable attend and chair any review meeting, take steps to ensure that such meetings are held in accordance with regulations; in particular that the child's views are understood and taken into account, that those responsible for implementing review decisions are identified and that any failure to properly review the case is brought to the attention of an appropriate senior person in the authority.

■ If the child whose case is reviewed wishes to take proceedings under the Act e.g. to apply to the court for contact or for discharge of a Care Order, the IRO must;

- Assist her/him to obtain legal advice or
- Establish whether an appropriate adult is able an willing to provide such assistance or bring the proceedings in the child's behalf

■ If an IRO does refer a case to CAFCASS under s.26 (2A) (c), the Children and Family Court Advisory and Support Service (Reviewed Case Referral) Regulations 2004 prescribe how CAFCASS must respond and state clearly that consideration must be given to the possibility of launching an action for judicial review or instituting a claim under the Human Rights Act 1998 for potential breaches of the articles of the ECHR.

General Duties toward Persons 'Qualifying for Advice and Assistance' [s.24 substituted by s.4 Children (Leaving Care) Act 2000 and amended by Sch.3 paras. 60 & 61 ACA 2002]

■ A person 'qualifying for advice and assistance' is now defined as a person:

- Aged 16 or over but under 21
- With respect to whom a Special Guardianship Order is in force (or was before s/he reached 18 years of age) and
- Who was, immediately before the making of that order, looked after by a local authority **or**
- Is under 21 and

- At any time between being 16 and before being 18 was looked after, accommodated or fostered

NB. Looked after, accommodated or fostered means here looked after by a local authority, accommodated by or on behalf of a voluntary organisation, accommodated in a private children's home or accommodated for a consecutive minimum period of 3 months by any health or special health authority, primary care trust (PCT) or local education authority (LEA) or in any care home, independent hospital or any accommodation provided by a NHS trust or privately fostered

■ In the case of a person looked after by a local authority, the duty falls to the last local authority which looked after her/him, to take such steps as it thinks necessary to discharge duties under s.24(1A) and s.24(1B) – described below.

■ For purposes of duties and powers in s.24 (general advice/assistance or associated with education/training/employment) the relevant local authority is:

- In the case of a person who was looked after, the local authority which last looked after her/him
- In any other case, the local authority within whose area person is (if s/he has asked for help of a sort which can be provided under s.24A or s.24B)

■ The relevant local authority must first decide:

- If a person qualifying for advice and assistance needs it and

- Where the person was not being looked after by a local authority, be satisfied whoever had been doing so does not have the necessary facilities

■ If the above 2 conditions are met, the local authority must advise and befriend the person if s/he was being looked after by a local authority or accommodated by or on behalf of a voluntary organisation, and may do so in any other case [s.24A (1)–(4) as amended by Children (Leaving Care) Act 2000 and Sch.3 paras.61 & 62 ACA 2002].

NB. Where the local authority is thus obliged or empowered, it may also provide assistance in kind and in exceptional circumstances assistance may be given by providing accommodation (if assistance can't be provided by virtue of s.24B), or in cash [s.24A (4)–(5) as amended by Children (Leaving Care) Act 2000 and s.116 ACA 2002].

■ The relevant local authority may give assistance to a person who 'qualifies for advice and assistance' by contributing to expenses incurred by her/him living near the place where s/he is working/seeking work [s.24B(1) as amended by Children (Leaving Care) Act 2000 and Sch.3 para.62 ACA 2002].

■ The relevant local authority may also give assistance to a person aged under 24 and does (or would, if under 21) qualify for advice and assistance by:

- Contributing to expenses incurred by the person living near the place s/he is or will be receiving education/training or

- Making a grant to enable her/him meet expenses connected to education/training [s.24B(2);(3) as amended by Children (Leaving Care) Act 2000]

NB. Where assisting a person with education/ training, the local authority may disregard interruptions of attendance if the course is resumed as soon as reasonably practicable.

- Where the local authority is satisfied a person entitled to advice and assistance described above and in full-time further (i.e. full-time residential) or higher education, needs vacation accommodation, it must assist by:

  - Providing suitable accommodation or
  - Paying the person enough to enable her/him to secure such accommodation [s.24B(5) as amended by Children (Leaving Care) Act 2000 & Reg.11(3) Children (Leaving Care) (England) Regulations 2001]

Additional Duties to 'Eligible', 'Relevant' & 'Former Relevant' Children [s. 22; s.23A–C; Sch.2 paras. 19B –19C; as amended/ introduced by Children (Leaving Care) Act 2000]

- The local authority has additional responsibilities for explicitly defined groups of 16 and 17 year olds who are, or who have been looked after as well as to those aged 18 or over who had been defined as belonging to one of those groups [see Leaving Care section below].

Leaving Care

Children (Leaving Care) Act 2000 & Children (Leaving Care) (England) Regulations 2001

■ A summary of these provisions is that they:

- Place a duty on local authorities to assess needs of 'eligible' and 'relevant' children
- Define 'eligible' children as those aged 16 or 17 who have been looked after for a period of 13 weeks continuously or in aggregate (with any period before age 14 excluded for purpose of aggregation)
- Define 'relevant' children as eligible young people of 16 or 17 who cease to be looked after (those returning home permanently or in receipt of short-breaks are excluded)
- Clarify that the 'responsible local authority' will be the one which last looked after the child
- Introduce a duty on the responsible local authority to keep in touch with all qualifying care leavers
- Oblige local authorities to formulate for all eligible and relevant children up to 21 years old regularly reviewed 'pathway plans' (replacing care plans), which cover education, training, career plan and the support needed
- Introduce 'personal advisers' for all eligible and relevant children to help draw up and support pathway plans and keep in touch with individuals

- Oblige local authorities in relevant cases, to assist care leavers in higher education with vacation accommodation
- Empower responsible local authorities to assist with costs of education and training up to age of twenty four, whenever a course may commence
- Place local authorities under a duty to financially support care leavers and remove entitlement from specified means-tested benefits from eligible and relevant young people.

NB. Regulations cited below apply in England. Those in Wales are comparable.

Child Eligible for After Care, Definition & Local Authority Duties

- A child is eligible for after care if s/he:

  - Is aged 16 or 17 and
  - Has been looked after by a local authority for a period/s totalling 13 weeks which began after s/he was 14 years old and ended when s/he had reached 16 years of age [Sch.2 para. 19B(2) CA 1989 introduced by s.1 Children (Leaving Care) Act 2000 and reg. 3(1) Children (Leaving Care) (England) Regulations 2001]

- In spite of meeting the above criteria, the child is **not** eligible for this service if:

  - The local authority has arranged to place her/him in a pre-planned series of short-term placements each of 4 weeks or fewer (even if these total 13) and

- At the end of each placement, the child returned to the care of a parent or a person with parental responsibility [para.19B (2) Children Act 1989 and reg. 3 Children (Leaving Care) (England) Regulations 2001 introduced by s.1 Children (Leaving Care) Act 2000].

■ The local authority must carry out an assessment of the needs of each eligible individual so as to determine what advice, assistance and support it would be appropriate to provide under the Children (Leaving Care) Act 2000:

- While the local authority is looking after her/him and
- After the local authority ceases to look after her/him

■ Based upon the above assessment, the local authority must then prepare a pathway plan for her/him [s.1 (4) Children (Leaving Care) Act 2000].

Conducting an Assessment for Purposes of Formulating Pathway Plans [Regs. 5 & 6 Children (Leaving Care) (England) Regulations 2001]

■ The responsible local authority must prepare a written statement describing the manner in which needs of each eligible and relevant child will be assessed [reg.5 (1) Children (Leaving Care) (England) Regulations 2001].

- The written statement must include information about in particular:

  - The person responsible for the conduct and co-ordination of the assessment
  - The timetable for the assessment
  - Who is to be consulted
  - Arrangements for recording the outcomes
  - Procedure for making representations in the event of disagreement [reg.5(2) Children (Leaving Care) (England) Regulations 2001]

- The responsible local authority must make a copy of the statement available to:

  - The child
  - Her/his parents
  - Any other person who has parental responsibility
  - Any person who on a day to day basis cares for or provides accommodation for her/him
  - Any college/school attended by her/him or the local education authority for the area in which s/he lives
  - Any independent visitor appointed for the person
  - Anyone providing health or treatment to her/him
  - The appointed personal adviser
  - Any other person whose views local authority or child may consider relevant [reg.5(3) & 7(5) Children (Leaving Care) (England) Regulations 2001]

■ The responsible local authority in carrying out an assessment and in preparing or reviewing a pathway must, unless it is not reasonable practicable:

- Seek and have regard to the views of the child to whom it relates and
- Take all reasonable steps to enable her/him to attend and participate in any meetings at which her/his case is to be considered [reg.6(1) Children (Leaving Care) (England) Regulations 2001]

■ The responsible local authority must also without delay provide the child with copies of the results of her/his assessment, pathway plan, each review of that plan and ensure the contents of each document are explained in accordance with her/his level of understanding, unless not reasonably practicable to do so [reg.6 (2) Children (Leaving Care) (England) Regulations 2001].

Timing & Content of Assessments [Reg. 7 Children (Leaving Care) Regulations (England) 2001]

■ The responsible local authority must assess the needs of each eligible and relevant child who does not already have a pathway plan as follows.

■ The assessment is to be completed:

- For an eligible child, not more than 3 months after s/he reaches the age of 16 or becomes an eligible child

- For a relevant child who does not already have a pathway plan, not more than 3 months after s/he becomes a relevant child [reg.7(2) Children (Leaving Care) (England) Regulations 2001]

■ Each responsible local authority must keep a written record of the:

- Information obtained in the course of the assessment
- Deliberations at any meeting held in connection with any aspect of the assessment and
- Results of assessment [reg.7(3) Children (Leaving Care) (England) Regulations 2001]

■ In carrying out its assessment the responsible local authority must take account of the following:

- Child's health and development
- Her/his need for education, training or employment
- The support available from members of her/his family and other persons
- The child's financial needs
- The extent to which s/he possesses the practical and other skills necessary for independent living
- The child's needs for care, support and accommodation [reg.7(4) Children (Leaving Care) (England) Regulations 2001]

■ The responsible local authority must also, unless it is not reasonably practicable to do so, take account of the views of:

- The parents of the child

- Any non-parent who has parental responsibility
- Any person who on a day to day basis, cares for or provides accommodation for the child
- Any school or college attended by the child or the LEA for the area in which s/he lives
- Any independent visitor appointed for the child
- Any person providing health care or treatment
- The appointed personal adviser
- Any other person whose views the local authority or child consider may be relevant [reg.7 (5) Children (Leaving Care) (England) Regulations 2001]

Meaning, Formulation & Review of Pathway Plans [s23E as introduced by s.3 Children (Leaving Care) Act 2000 & Regs. 8 & 9 Children (Leaving Care) (England) Regulations 2001]

■ A pathway plan is a plan setting out, for:

- Eligible children, the advice, assistance and support which the local authority intends to provide while it is looking after the person and later (including when s/he may cease to be looked after) and for
- Relevant children, the advice, assistance and support the local authority intends to provide under Part III [s.23E as inserted by s.3 Children (Leaving Care) Act 2000]

■ The pathway plan must be prepared as soon as possible after the assessment and must in particular include:

- Nature and level of contact and personal support to be provided and by whom to the child
- Details of the accommodation for her/him
- A detailed plan for education or training
- How the responsible local authority will assist in relation to employment or other purposeful activity or occupation
- Support to be provided to enable the child to develop and sustain appropriate family and social relationships
- A programme to develop practical and other skills necessary for living independently
- Financial support to be provided in particular where it is to be provided to meet accommodation and maintenance needs
- Health needs, including (mental health) needs of child and how they are to be met
- Contingency plans for action by the responsible local authority should the pathway plan for any reason cease to be effective [schedule to Children (Leaving Care) (England) Regulations 2001]

■ For both eligible and relevant children, the pathway plan must set out in writing, the:

- Manner in which the local authority proposes to meet the needs of the child
- Date by which and by whom, any action required to implement any aspect of the plan will be carried out [reg.8(1)-(3) Children (Leaving Care) (England) Regulations 2001]

■ The responsible local authority must review the pathway plan of eligible, relevant and former relevant children:

  • If requested to do so by the child
  • If it, or the personal adviser considers a review necessary and
  • In any other case, at intervals of no more than 6 months [reg.9(1) & (2) Children (Leaving Care) (England) Regulations 2001]

■ The local authority must, to the extent it considers appropriate, seek and take account of views of:

  • The parents of the child
  • Any non-parent who has parental responsibility
  • Any person who on a day to day basis, cares for or provides accommodation for the child
  • Any school or college attended by the child or the LEA for the area in which s/he lives
  • Any independent visitor appointed for the child
  • Any person providing health care or treatment
  • The personal adviser appointed for the child
  • Any other person whose views local authority or child consider may be relevant [reg.9(3) Children (Leaving Care) (England) Regulations 2001]

■ The local authority may carry out such reviews at same time as s.26 CA 1989 reviews [s.1 (6) Children (Leaving Care) Act 2000] and outputs must be recorded [reg.9 (5) Children (Leaving Care) (England) Regulations 2001].

NB. Failure to involve a child of 16 or over will be a

breach of Article 6 of the European Convention – see Re M (Care Challenging Decisions by Local Authority) [2001] 2 FLR 1300 in which a failure to involve the parents of a child in a permanency planning meeting was regarded as such.

Personal Advisers

■ The local authority must arrange for each eligible child whom it is looking after to have a personal adviser [sch.2 para.19C introduced by s.1 Children (Leaving Care) Act 2000].

■ The functions of the personal adviser are to:

- Provide advice, including practical advice and support
- Where applicable, participate in assessment, and preparation of the pathway plan
- Participate in the review of the pathway plan
- Liaise with the responsible local authority in the implementation of the plan
- Co-ordinate service provision and take reasonable steps to ensure s/he makes use of such services
- Keep informed about her/his progress and well-being and
- Keep a record of contacts [reg.12 Children (Leaving Care) (England) Regulations 2001]

NB. In R(J) v Caerphilly County Borough Council [2005] EWHC 586(Admin), it was concluded that although it was not unlawful to appoint as a

*personal adviser, an employee of the young person's
local authority, the assessment and pathway plan
must be completed by someone other than the
personal adviser whose role is distinct.*

Relevant Child & Local Authority Duties

■ A relevant child [s.23A Children Act 1989
introduced by s.2 Children (Leaving Care) Act 2000
and reg. 4 Children (Leaving Care) (England)
Regulations 2001] is one aged 16 or 17 who:

  • Is not being looked after by any local authority
  • Was, before ceasing to be looked after, an
    eligible child for purposes described above
  • Is not subject to a Care Order

■ A child is also defined as relevant if, as well as
satisfying above criteria, and whilst 16 or over, s/he
was (having immediately before
admission/detention been looked after for a`
period/s totalling at least 13 weeks starting after
the age of 14):

  • Detained in a remand centre, young offender
    institution (YOI), secure training centre (STC) or
    other court-ordered institution, or
  • In a hospital

■ In calculating 13 weeks, no account is taken of any
period in which child was looked after by a local
authority in any of a pre-planned series of short-term
placements each of 4 weeks or fewer, at the end of
which s/he returned to care of a parent or person

with parental responsibility [para.19B (2) Children Act 1989 and reg. 3 Children (Leaving Care) (England) Regulations 2001 introduced by s.1 Children (Leaving Care) Act 2000].

■ Unless arrangement breaks down and s/he ceases to live with that person, a child in a 'family placement' for a continuous period of 6 months or more (whether or not period began whilst looked after) is not a 'relevant child' [s.23A (1)-(3) Children Act 1989 and Regulation 4 &5 Children (Leaving Care) (England) Regulations 2001 introduced by s.1 Children (Leaving Care) Act 2000].

■ Each local authority must take reasonable steps to keep in touch with a relevant child for whom it is responsible whether s/he is within its area or not [s.23B (1) introduced by s.2 Children (Leaving Care) Act 2000].

■ If it has not already appointed one whilst the individual was an eligible child, the local authority must appoint a personal adviser for each relevant child [s.23B (2) introduced by s.2 Children (Leaving Care) Act 2000].

■ If a pathway plan has not already been formulated, the local authority must assess need and prepare one [s.23B (3) introduced by s.2 Children (Leaving Care) Act 2000].

NB. This assessment may be done at the same time as any other one e.g. special needs or disability-related.

■ The local authority must review its pathway plan regularly [s.23B (7) introduced by s.2 Children (Leaving Care) Act 2000].

■ The local authority must safeguard and promote the relevant child's welfare and unless satisfied that her/his welfare does not require it, must offer support by:

- Maintaining her/him
- Providing, or maintaining her/him in suitable accommodation
- Providing support of such other descriptions as may be prescribed (support is assistance to meet education, training or employment needs as provided for in pathway plan [Reg.11 Children (Leaving Care) (England) Regulations 2001] and may be in cash)

■ Suitable accommodation means accommodation:

- Which, so far as reasonably practicable is suitable for the child in the light of her/his needs including health and any needs arising from any disability
- In respect of which the responsible local authority has satisfied itself as to the character and suitability of the landlord or other provider

NB. In the case of Bluett v Suffolk County Council and others [2005] 1 FCR 89 the Court of Appeal allowed an appeal against the dismissal of a girl's claim in negligence against the local authority for the decision by her social worker to advise her to go into accommodation which was known to be materially insecure and where there was a known risk of dangerously violent incursions by intruders. Following a prolonged invasion of the hostel, the girl had been subject to invasion of her room and had jumped from her bedroom window in order to escape thereby suffering permanently incapacitating injuries. The Court of Appeal ruled that the claimant had a pleadable case against the local authority as a result of the failures of the social worker.

- In respect of which the local authority has, so far as is reasonably practical taken into account the child's wishes/feelings and education, training and employment needs [Reg.11(2) Children (Leaving Care) (England) Regulations 2001]

■ If the local authority has lost touch with a relevant child, it must without delay:

- Consider how to re-establish contact
- Take reasonable steps to do so
- Continue efforts for as long as s/he is a relevant child (up to 18 years) until it succeeds [s23B(11) introduced by s.2 Children (Leaving Care) Act 2000]

■ The local authority has the same duty to ascertain and take account of wishes/feelings of child, parents and others as in its s.22 duties toward those who are being or may be looked after [s23B(13) introduced by s.2 Children (Leaving Care) Act 2000].

Responsible Authority

■ The responsible authority for purposes of a relevant child is the one which last looked after a child [s.23A (4) CA 1989 introduced by s.2 (4) Children (Leaving Care) Act 2000].

NB. This changes the previous arrangements whereby the local authority within which the child was resident was responsible for service provision and so reverses one aspect of the decision in R v London Borough of Lambeth ex parte Cadell [1998] 1 FLR 253.

Former Relevant Child [s.23C as Introduced by Children (Leaving Care) Act 2000]

■ With respect to a person aged 18 or over, who had been a relevant or eligible child, the local authority which was last the responsible local authority is obliged to:

- Take reasonable steps to keep in touch with the former relevant child whether s/he is in the local authority area or not
- Re-establish contact if it loses touch with the individual
- Continue the appointment of a personal adviser
- Continue to review pathway plan regularly

■ The local authority must also give a former relevant child aged up to 21 years old, to the extent that her/his:

- Welfare requires it, advice and assistance by means of contributing to expenses incurred by living near the place of actual/potential employment
- Welfare and educational or training needs requires it, contributions to expenses incurred by living near the place of actual/potential education/training, or grants for expenses connected with education/training

NB. This support may continue beyond the age of 21 and may be transferred to another local authority if the young person moves to a new one (see R v London Borough of Lambeth ex parte Cadell [1998] 1 FLR 253).

■ The local authority must also, to the extent that her/his welfare requires it, give other assistance which may be in kind or in exceptional circumstances cash.

■ The duties described above generally apply until the former relevant child is 21 years old [s.23C (6) introduced by s.2 Children (Leaving Care) Act 2000].

■ If though, the pathway plan sets out a programme of education/training which extends beyond her/his 21st birthday, then the duties associated with that programme continue for as long as the former relevant child pursue that programme [s.23C(7)(a) introduced by s.2 Children (Leaving Care) Act 2000].

NB. Any interruption in pursuance of education/training programmes must be disregarded

*if the local authority satisfied that the former
relevant child will resume it as soon as reasonably
practicable [s.23C(8) introduced by s.2 Children
(Leaving Care) Act 2000].*

■ A consequent duty if an individual's
education/training programme continues beyond
21, is local authority must keep in touch, maintain a
personal adviser and continue to review pathway
plan [s.23C (7) (b) introduced by s.2 Children
(Leaving Care) Act 2000].

Retention & Confidentiality of Records [Reg.10 Children (Leaving Care) (England) Regulations 2001]

■ Records relating to assessments, pathway plans and
their review must be retained by the responsible
local authority until the subject is 75 years old.

*NB. If the individual dies before18, the records must
be kept for 15 years after her/his death.*

■ The above records may be written originals, copies,
or in whole or in part on computer so long as
accessible, kept securely and not disclosed to any
person except in accordance with any relevant law or
a court order.

*NB. Failure to keep such records intact and provide
access by child to them, may constitute a denial of
individual's right to private and family life under
Article 8 of the European Convention seen in Gaskin
v UK [1990] 1 FLR 167.*

Transfer of Information about Care Leavers [s.24C as amended by Children (Leaving Care) Act 2000]

■ Where it appears to a local authority that a person specified in s.24 with whom it has a duty to keep in touch, whom it has been advising or befriending or to whom it has been giving assistance, proposes to live or is living in the area of another local authority, it must inform that authority [s.24C (1) as introduced by Children (Leaving Care) Act 2000].

■ If any one of the following organisations cease to accommodate a child aged 16 or over, it must notify the local authority in whose area s/he proposes to live:

  • A voluntary organisation or private children's home after any period of time or
  • (Assuming a consecutive period of 3 months or more) any health authority, special health authority, primary care trust or local education authority, or any care home, independent hospital or any accommodation provided by a NHS trust [s.24C(2) as amended by Children (Leaving Care) Act 2000].

Exclusion from Benefits [s.6 Children (Leaving Care) Act 2000]

■ An eligible or relevant child (who by definition is aged less than 18) is not entitled to:

  • Income Based Job-seekers allowance

- Income Support or
- Housing Benefit

NB. S.6 (3) enables the Secretary of State to make regulations to ensure that particular groups are not included e.g. care leavers who are lone parents or disabled.

There is no provision to remove non-means tested benefits such as Disability Living Allowance which will continue to be paid to any care leavers who qualify for them.

There is no reference to Council Tax because under 18 year olds are not liable to pay it.

Secure Accommodation for Looked After Children [s.25]

- A looked after child can be placed and kept in secure accommodation only if s/he:

  - Has a history of absconding, and
  - Is likely to abscond from anywhere else, and
  - Is likely, when absconding, to suffer significant harm, or
  - Kept elsewhere, is likely to injure self or others

- The local authority must apply to court for a Secure Accommodation Order and child should be legally represented in accordance with the child's Article 6 rights.

  NB. In Re C [2001] 1 FLR 169 these rights were found not to have been violated even though C's solicitor was only informed of the application for a s.25 order on arrival at court.

- The placement must be reviewed at least every 28 days and include an independent element.

- An accommodated child could be placed in security, but parent/s and those with parental responsibility would have a right to remove her/him.

- A child of under 13 cannot be placed in secure accommodation in a children's home without the prior approval of the Secretary of State.

  NB. The local authority has discretion to place a

child in security for a maximum of 72 hours in 28 days. Children's Guardians will be appointed as per s.41.

- The High Court has held that s.25 applications can be considered even where a child is already detained under another statutory power e.g. Mental Health Act 1983.

- The wording of the Children Act 1989 and Reg.5 of the Secure Accommodation Regs. 1991 should be interpreted to mean it is not necessary for the provisions of s.25 also to be satisfied in the case of a detained child [Hereford & Worcester County Council v S Family Division [1993] 2 FLR 360].

- The Court of Appeal has decided neither 'welfare' or 'positive advantage' principles apply, so if the court has found any of s.25 or regulation 6 criteria are satisfied, it must make an Order [Re M (Secure Accommodation Order) [1995] 1 FLR 418].

- In Re K (Secure Accommodation Order: Right to Liberty) (Court of Appeal; Dame Elizabeth Butler-Sloss P, Thorpe and Judge LJJ; 15 November 2000, the Court concluded a Secure Accommodation Order is not incompatible with Article 5 of the Convention (Right To Liberty and Security of Person) because it is justified within Article 5(1) (d) as the detention of a minor for the purpose of 'educational supervision'. The latter term should not be equated rigidly with notions of classroom teaching, and particularly in a care context should embrace many aspects of the exercise of parental rights for the benefit and protection of the child concerned.

Remands to Secure Accommodation [s.25 (7)]

■ Subject to specified conditions, a court remanding a male or female aged twelve to fourteen, or a female aged fifteen or sixteen to local authority accommodation may, after consultation with the designated authority require that authority to comply with a security requirement i.e. that the child be placed and kept in secure accommodation [s.23 (4) CYPA 1969 as substituted by s.60 CJA 1991 and amended by s.97 (1) CDA 1998].

■ Criteria for imposition of a security requirement are that:

- The individual is charged with or convicted of a violent or sexual offence or an offence punishable in the case of an adult with imprisonment for a term of 14 years more **or**
- S/he is charged with or has been convicted of one or more imprisonable offences which, together with any other imprisonable offences of which s/he has been convicted in any proceedings amount (or would amount if s/he were convicted of the offences with which s/he is charged) to a recent history of repeatedly committing imprisonable offences while remanded on bail or to local authority accommodation **and in addition,**
- The court is of the opinion, after considering all

the options for the remand of the individual, that only a secure remand would be adequate either to protect the public from serious harm from her/him **or** to prevent the commission by her/him of imprisonable offences [s.23(5AA) Children and Young Persons' Act 1969 as amended by s.130(3) Criminal Justice and Police Act 2001]

NB. Serious harm is defined in s.161 Powers of Criminal Courts (Sentencing) Act 2000 in relation to sexual and violent offences as 'death or serious personal injury, whether physical or psychological, occasioned by further such offences committed by him'. It is not defined in relation to other offences.

Further details as to the required conditions for imposition of a security requirement and of the special measure for specified males aged 15 and 16 are contained in CAE's Personal Guide to The Crime and Disorder Act 1998 [see appendix 3]

In Re G (Secure Accommodation Order) Family Division; Munby J [2001]1 FLR 884, the court concluded a Youth Court does have jurisdiction to apply the usual criteria of s.25(1) if it is dealing with a child remanded/committed to local authority accommodation.

Complaints & Representations Procedure [ss.26 & 24D as introduced by s.5 Children (Leaving Care) Act 2000]

■ The local authority must establish a procedure for considering any representations (including complaints) made to it about the discharge of any functions under Part III of the Act (i.e. Family Support Services) by:

- Any child looked after or in need
- A child qualifying for advice and assistance
- An eligible or relevant child
- A former relevant child
- Such a child's parent or someone with parental responsibility
- A local authority foster carer
- Such other person as the local authority considers has sufficient interest in the child's welfare,

■ In R v Kingston-upon-Thames Royal Borough ex parte T [1994] 1 FLR 798 it was held that anyone with a grievance should, prior to seeking judicial review, use the s.26 procedures. This was confirmed as the correct approach in R v Birmingham City Council ex parte A [1997] 2 FLR 841.

NB. An applicant in a judicial review must generally show the local authority has acted in a way in which no reasonable authority would have acted (see R v Lancashire CC ex parte M [1992] 1 FLR 109).

Where a complaints panel includes representatives of the local authority, this could be argued to be contrary to Article 6 of the Convention (Right To A Fair Trial Including An Independent and Impartial Tribunal) as in R on the application of Christopher Beeson v Dorset CC and the Secretary of State for Health [200] EWCHA 986 30 November 2001.

s.26 CA 1989 has been amended by s.117 ACA 2002 to extend the scope of complaints and representations procedure to include those functions of Part 4 and 5 of the Children Act 1989 to be specified by the Secretary of State in regulations as well as functions relating to the adoption service offered by the local authority.

Representations & Complaints by Care Leavers [Reg.13 Children (Leaving Care) (England) Regulations 2001 & s.117 ACA 2002]

■ The following persons are entitled to make a representation/complaint about 'qualifying functions' (family support services and specified duties in the care/supervision and child protection provisions of the Children Act 1989) :

- A child 'qualifying for advice/assistance'
- An 'eligible child'
- A 'relevant child' and
- An individual for whose needs provision is made

in the ACA 2002, or such other person the local authority consider has sufficient interest

■ If a local authority receives such a representation/ complaint, it must:

- Provide the local authority officer who has responsibility for such matters with a written summary of that representation/complaint
- Endeavour by informal means to reach a settlement to the satisfaction of the complainant within 14 days and
- If at the end of 14 days no resolution has been reached, notify the local authority officer of that fact [Reg. 3A (1) The Representations Procedure(Children) Regulations 1991]

NB. Provisions in Wales are essentially comparable.

Special Guardianship Order Support Services: Representations [14G Children Act 1989]

■ Every local authority is obliged to establish a procedure for considering representations (including complaints) made to it by any person to whom it may provide special guardianship support services about the discharge of its functions under s.14 F (1) in relation to her/him [s.14G(1) Children Act 1989 inserted by ACA 2002].

■ The Children Act 1989 Representations Procedure (England)Regulations 2006 Regulations have been made by the Secretary of State pursuant to s.14G (2) Children Act 1989 (inserted by ACA 2002), providing for such procedures to be in place in relation to any functions associated with the provision of special guardianship support services (see reg 5)and imposing under reg 9(1) a time limit of 1 year on the making of the above representations, but the regulations go on to provide that a local authority may consider any representations outside the time limit if, having regard to all the circumstances, it concludes that: it would not be reasonable to expect the complainant to have made the representations within the time limit (reg 9(2)(a)) and notwithstanding the time that has passed, it is still possible to consider the representations effectively and fairly (reg ((2)(b).

Advocacy Service [s.26A introduced by s.119 ACA 2002]

■ Every local authority must make arrangements for the provision of assistance (including representation) to children or care leavers wishing to use s.26 s.24D respectively to make complaints or representations

■ The Advocacy Services and Representations Procedure (Children) (Amendment) Regulations 2004 SI 719 specify that persons who may **not** provide **such** assistance are those who:

- Are or may be the subject of the representations
- Are responsible for managing the person who is or may be the subject of the representations
- Manage the service which is or may be the subject of the representations

- Have control over the resources allocated to the service which is or may be the subject of the representation

■ Local authorities are obliged to provide a potential or actual complainant with information about advocacy services and offer help in obtaining an advocate.

■ Local authorities must also monitor compliance with the requirements of these regulations.

NB. Provisions in Wales are essentially comparable.

Part IV: Care and Supervision

Care and Supervision

Duty to Protect Child

■ The proper response to a child thought to be at risk of significant harm is Part IV, **not** s.8 [Nottinghamshire County Council v P [1993] 2 FLR 134].

Attendance of Child at Court

■ Attendance is at court's discretion [s.95].

■ Court may ask for advice from a children's guardian.

NB. Article 6 of the Convention (Right To a Fair Trial) could be argued to justify child's presence in court.

Applications & Grounds

■ An application may be made only by a local authority or N.S.P.C.C. with respect to a child up to her/his seventeenth birthday (16th if married) who is suffering or likely to suffer 'significant harm' where the harm, or likelihood of harm, is attributable to the care given, or likely to be given to child, not being what it would be reasonable to expect a parent to give her/him, or child is beyond parental control.

■ The House of Lords has previously determined that the critical date for satisfying the threshold conditions above is the date upon which the local authority initiate protective proceedings [Re M (A Minor) (Care Order: Threshold Conditions) [1994] 2 FLR 377].

- Re G (Care Proceedings: Threshold Conditions) Re [2001] 2 FLR 1111, suggests that evidence gathering after the initiation of proceedings and later acquired information as to the state of affairs at the time proceedings were initiated, could be taken into account by a court.

- In Re C and B (Care Order: Future Harm) [2001] 1 FLR 611, the Court of Appeal emphasised the principle of proportionality in Article 8 of the European Convention required that action taken by a local authority must be a proportionate response to the feared harm.

- In the above case, 2 older children of the family had been made subject of Care Orders in 1996. After a report from an independent social worker assessing that these facts disclosed a risk to the 3rd child then aged 10 months and doing well in the care of its mother, the local authority applied for an Emergency Protection Order on the 4th child on the day of its birth and an interim order on the 3rd child. The Court of Appeal found that the local authority had not taken the time to explore alternative options and that its actions were not proportionate.

- The House of Lords has ruled that in interpreting the phrase 'the care given to the child', that phrase refers primarily to the care given by parent/s or other primary carers, but where care is shared, the phrase can embrace the care given by **any** of the carers. This interpretation was necessary to allow the Court to intervene to protect a child who was clearly at risk, even though it was not possible to identify the source of the risk [Lancashire CC v B [2000] 1 FLR 583].In addition, it has been decided by the House of Lords in Re O and N and Re B[[2003] 1 FLR 1169] that where it was impossible to tell which of 2 parents had inflicted the injuries or whether both had done so, then the threshold criteria were met.

NB. Where a child suffered significant harm but the court was unable to identify which parent had been the perpetrator, or indeed, whether both had been, the court should proceed at the welfare stage on the footing that each parent was a possible perpetrator i.e. it would be wrong, if, because neither parent had been proved to be the perpetrator, the court had to proceed as the welfare stage as though child was not at risk from either parent even though one or other of them was the perpetrator of significant harm [Re O and N; Re B [2–3] 1 FLR 1169 HL]

Definition of 'Harm'

■ 'Harm' is defined as: ill treatment (including sexual and non-physical abuse) or impairment of health (physical or mental) or development (physical, intellectual, emotional, social or behavioural), including for example impairment suffered from seeing or hearing the ill-treatment of another [s.31 as amended by s.120 ACA 2002].

■ 'Significant' in relation to health or development is: In comparison to what could reasonably be expected of a similar child.

- In Re O (A Minor) (Care Order: Education Procedure) [1992] 2 FLR 7 it was found that the relevant comparison was with a child of similar intellectual and social development who has gone to school, not with an average child who may or may not have attended properly.

- In a case heard by the House of Lords, Re H and R (Child Sexual Abuse: Standards of Proof) [1996] 1 FLR 80, L.R., it was determined that:

  - In s.31(2) 'likelihood of harm' is established if, court concludes is a real or substantial risk of significant harm in future (harm does not have to be shown as being more probable than not)
  - The required standard of proof for an allegation of sexual abuse is balance of probabilities, taking account of the fact that the more improbable the event, the stronger must be the evidence that it **did** occur, before on the balance of probability, its occurrence would be established

  NB. This approach has been confirmed as being the correct one in the Court of Appeal decisions in Re U and Re B [2004] 2 FLR 263, which followed on the case of Angela Cannings, and rejected the suggestion made by Bodey J in Re ET [2003] 2FLR 1205 that the difference between the civil and criminal standards of proof was largely illusory.

  - In order to rely upon past events to establish the threshold criteria these facts must be proved to the required standard

NB. One could argue that the above also applies to fabricated or induced illness.

Care Plans [s.31 (3A)]

■ No Care Order may be made until the court has considered a 's.31A plan' (care plan).

■ Where a full Care Order might be made, the appropriate local authority i.e. the one to be designated in any order, must, within a time-scale directed by the court, laid down now in the Protocol for Judicial Case Management in Public Law Children Act Cases [2003] 2 FLR 719, which **must be followed by all parties to the case, including the local authority**) prepare a plan.

■ While the application is pending, the authority must keep its s.31A plan under review and revise it as the authority consider necessary

Twin-Track Planning

■ In Re D and Another (Children) (Care Plan: Twin Track Planning) [1999] 4 All ER, Bracewell J. stated that in order to prevent delays in providing permanency, it is incumbent on local authorities and children's guardians to identify clearly the options available for the court by 'twin track' planning, rather than the conventional sequential approach.

■ The 'Handbook of Best Practice in Children Act Cases' published by the then Children Act Advisory Committee in 1997 stated...' if the plan is for an adoptive placement, the court will be handicapped in assessing the plan and times-scale unless the child concerned has already been considered and approved by the adoption and fostering panel and potential suitable adoptive families have been identified. It is not good practice to await the making of a Care Order before obtaining such information'.

NB. LAC (99)29 provided guidance on 'Care Plans and Care Proceedings. The 'Protocol for Judicial Case Management in Public Law Cases' must be followed with effect from 01.11.03 and LAC (04)1 provides further guidance.

Human Rights

■ In Home Office Human Rights Act 1998 'Core Guidance' it is suggested the principle of 'proportionality' used by the European Court requires that if action is taken breaching the right to family life under Article 8(1) which is then justified by reference to Article 8(2), such action must be proportionate to the end set out in Article 8(2).

■ The Core Guidance paraphrases this as 'not taking a sledgehammer to crack a nut' and the example given of proportionality is that of Care Proceedings.

■ In Re O (Supervision Order) [2001] 1 FLR 923, in the Court of Appeal, the importance of 'proportionality' of intervention was reinforced where an appeal by a local authority against a refusal to make a Care Order was dismissed and a Supervision Order confirmed as adequate for the particular circumstances.

NB. An allegation made in care proceedings that a local authority has breached the ECHR should be dealt with in those care proceedings (Re V [2004)]1 FLR 944.

Effects/ Duration of Care Order [ss.33; 34 as amended by Sch.3 paras. 63; 64 ACA 2002]

■ A Care Order:

- Gives the local authority parental responsibility and the right to decide to what extent parent, guardian, special guardian or a person who has parental responsibility by virtue of s.4A can meet their continuing parental responsibility
- Lasts until child is 18

NB. This may be argued to be in breach of the child's right to family life under Article 8(1)

- Discharges any existing Supervision Order (S.O.), Education Supervision (E.S.O.), s.8, School Attendance Order and, if child a Ward of Court, that Wardship
- Assumes contact with parent/s, guardian or special guardian, previous holders of Residence Orders, anyone who has parental responsibility by virtue of s.4A or persons with care of child by virtue of Order under High Court's inherent jurisdiction and the local authority 'contact plan' will be considered before a Care Order is made

■ On an application by those cited immediately above or others (with leave of court), the court may direct contact arrangements. [See also Local Authority General Duties to Looked After Children].

Court's Oversight of Proposed Care Plans

■ In Re: W and B (Care Plan) [2001] FLR 582, the Court of Appeal concluded that to avoid the Children Act being held incompatible with Articles 6 and 8 of the Convention, its interpretation would have to be modified.

■ Judges in Care Proceedings should have a wider discretion to make an interim Care Order [see below] or to defer making a Care Order where the Care Plan is 'inchoate' (unfinished or rudimentary) or where there are uncertainties capable of resolution.

■ 'Essential milestones' in the care plan should be collaboratively assessed, elevated to star status and a failure to achieve one within a reasonable time of the date set at trail should prompt the local authority to inform the child's guardian (so that s/he or the local authority might apply to the court for directions).

■ An appeal against the above judgement by the Secretary of State for Health and Bedfordshire County Council was heard in the House of Lords, Re S (Minors) (Care Order: Implementation of Care Plan); Re W(Minors) (Care Order: Adequacy of Care Plan) [2002] UKHL 10 where it was judged that:

- The court's introduction of a starring system was **not** a legitimate interpretation of the Children Act
- The Children Act itself was **not** incompatible with the European Convention for the Protection of Human Rights and Fundamental Freedoms 1950
- There **was** a gap in the law with respect to redress when a local authority was unable or unwilling to implement a care plan (now referred to as a s.31A plan)

NB. The introduction in s.118 ACA 2002 of an independent person to participate in a child's periodic s.26 review and refer the case to CAFCASS (for return to court) if s/he considers it appropriate, offers some opportunity for judicial oversight of inadequately implemented s.31A plans and s.26(2) (f) care plan (see page 108).

Limiting/Refusing Contact for Child In Care [s.34 & Contact with Children Regs. 1991]

Contact Plan [s.34 (2); (3)]

■ Courts must, before making a Care Order, consider and invite parties to comment upon, the proposed contact arrangements between child and parents and other involved relatives [s.34 (11)].

NB. Routine acceptance by courts of the local authority's proposals or of 'contact at the discretion of the local authority' could be argued to be breach of Article 8 of the Convention.

■ Directions as to contact may be given on the court's initiative or as a response to an application made by

- The local authority
- The child
- Parent/guardian/special guardian/person with parental responsibility by virtue of s.4A
- A person who either held a Residence Order or had care of the child by virtue of an order made under the High Court's inherent jurisdiction, immediately before the Care Order was made
- Any other person who has obtained the court's permission

NB. Contact may be by means of letters, e-mails, text messages, telephone, photographs or any other method as well as visits.

Local authorities are empowered to help with the cost of visiting looked after children where there would otherwise be undue hardship [sch.2 para.1].

Planned Refusal of Contact [s.34 (4)]

■ In response to an application by the local authority or child, the court may make an order which allows the local authority to refuse contact between the child and any of the persons listed in the contact plan section above.

■ Orders under s.34 can be made at the same time the Care Order is made or later, and may be varied or discharged on the application of the local authority, child or the person named in the order.

Emergency Refusal of Contact [s.34 (6)]

■ A local authority can refuse to allow the usual 'reasonable contact' or that which has been directed by the court if:

- It is satisfied that it is necessary to do so to safeguard and promote the child's welfare and
- The refusal is urgent and does not last more than 7 days.

■ When a local authority has decided to refuse contact in this way, it must immediately provide written notification to the following persons :

- The child (if of sufficient understanding)
- Parents or guardian/special guardian/person with parental responsibility by virtue of s.4A

- Anyone who immediately before Care Order
  made held a Residence Order or had care by
  virtue of order made under High Court's
  inherent jurisdiction and
- Anyone else whose wishes and feelings they
  consider relevant.

■ Notification must contain as much of the following
  as the local authority believes these persons need:

- The decision and the date it was made
- Reasons for the decision, and, if applicable
- How long it will last (max. 7 days)
- How to challenge the decision if dissatisfied

**Departure from Terms of Court Order about
Contact under s.34 [Reg.3 Contact Regs.]**

■ A local authority can depart from the terms of a
  court order if the person named in the order agrees
  and:

- Where the child is of sufficient understanding
  s/he also agrees
- Written notification was sent within 7 days

**Other Variations or Suspension of Contact
Arrangements [Reg.4 Contact Regs.]**

■ Where a local authority vary or suspend contact
  arrangements other than those made as result of a
  court order under s.34 , to allow a person contact
  with a child in care it must also provide written
  notification.

■ The High Court has determined s.34 is sufficiently wide to enable a court to make, effectively an interim Contact Order at the same time as a Care Order with specific provision for a further hearing with a view to making more enduring arrangements.[Re B (A Minor) (Care Order: Review) [1993] 1 FLR 421].

NB. Where the court concurs with the local authority view there should be no contact with a child, it should make no order for contact because such an action would confer no advantage on the local authority [Kent CC v. C 1993 Fam. 557].

■ In Re T (Termination of Contact: Discharge of Order [1997] 1 FLR 517 CA), the Court of Appeal considered in what circumstances a court should discharge an order made under s.34(4) authorising a local authority to refuse contact to a child in care and determined that:

- On an application to discharge, the court should not re-investigate propriety of original order
- Applicant must ...'as a threshold test , show circumstances have changed sufficiently to make application a genuine one'
- Once that test is satisfied, court should determine the application pursuant to s.1 Children Act 1989
- If, on the facts at the Hearing of such an application a s.34(4) order would not be justified then it should be discharged

■ The court also suggested making such an order would not be right unless is no realistic possibility of child's rehabilitation with person in question, a probable need to terminate contact is foreseeable and not too remote.

NB. Failure to consider the position of all those who might potentially have a contact relationship with a child e.g. an uncle, has successfully been argued to breach both uncle and child's rights under Article 8(1) of the Convention in Boyle v UK [1994] 19 EHRR 179.

Effects/ Duration of Supervision Order [s.35; Sch.3 parts 1 & 2]

■ A Supervision Order

- Requires supervisor to advise, assist and befriend
- Lasts 12 months, can be varied by court to a Care Order, discharged, or renewed to max of 3 years
- Imposes obligations on 'responsible person' (i.e. person with parental responsibility or with whom child living) to take reasonable steps to ensure compliance of child with Supervision Order and that s/he also complies with directions given

NB. The High Court has ruled that the construction of paras 2 & 3 of Sch.3 permits a court to direct that a 'responsible person' live with a child in a particular place [Croydon London Borough Council v A (No. 3) Family Division 03.07.92]. However the Act suggests

*that it is the Supervisor, not the court, who has
authority to direct and this determination, begs the
question of the responsible person's refusal to
consent!*

Interim Orders [s.38]

■ If a court has 'reasonable grounds' for believing
Care/Supervision criteria are met, an Interim Order
may be made:

- 1st interim may be up to 8 weeks
- 2nd and subsequent interim may be up to 4 weeks
  or the balance of the original 8 if that is longer

■ Contact rights in Interim Care Orders are same as a
full Care Order and a challenge would be via s.34.

■ No court may include in a Supervision Order a
requirement for psychiatric or medical examination
or treatment unless it is satisfied child has sufficient
understanding and consents (cf. Interim Supervision
Order; Care Order; Emergency Protection Order and
Child Assessment Order where the onus is on
medical/social work staff to determine sufficient
understanding) [Sch. 3 paras. 4; 5].

■ When a court dismisses application for a Care
Order/Supervision Order or grants an application for
discharge it may make a 'pending appeal' Care or
Supervision Order which may include specific
directions to safeguard child e.g. Lancashire CC v B
2000 FLR 583 by the Judge at first instance in the
County Court.

NB. A direction made under s.38 (6) by magistrates is subject to appeal to the High Court [Re O (Minor) (Medical Examinations) [1993] 1 FLR 860].

- In Re L (Interim Care Order: Power of Court) [1996] 2 FLR 742, the High Court concluded:

  - An Interim Care Order is a holding order which should not be treated as an indication of final disposal
  - An Interim Care Order **is** a Care Order, so the court has no more power to impose conditions or give directions (except for its statutory rights under s.38(6) to direct a medical examination or other assessment) than it would under a full order

- In Re C (Interim Care Order: Residential Assessment) [1997] 1 FLR 1 HL, the House of Lords reflected a narrow interpretation of s.38(6) which provides 'where the court makes an Interim Care or Supervision Order, it may make such directions (if any) as it considers appropriate with regard to the medical/psychiatric examination or other assessment of the child...'

- It was held that in many cases what is at issue is the risk to the child from her/his parents or other carers and that assessment of the child (especially if very young) is meaningless without assessment of the carers.

NB. This has cost implications for local authorities directed to undertake expensive and possibly futile assessment. In Berkshire County Council v C and Others [1993] 1 FLR 569 it was concluded a court considering making a direction with substantial financial implications for a local authority should approach this with particular care.

■ In Re M (Residential Assessment Directions) [1998] 2 FLR 371 the Judge suggested the following 4 relevant criteria, if fulfilled, justify exercise of the court's discretion about need to order such an assessment, i.e. it must:

- Be assessment as opposed to treatment
- Not be contrary to the child's overall best interests
- Be 'necessary' [as per Re: C case cited above]
- Not be unreasonable to expect local authority to be involved with and if ordered, fund assessment (thus the local authority should be allowed to adduce evidence or make representations)

NB. The above case should no longer be treated as a guideline case according to the Court of Appeal in Re G (Interim Care Order: Residential Assessment) [2004] EWCA Civ. 24 and the interpretation of the House of Lords in Re: C cited above was to be preferred.

*On a further appeal to the House of Lords (Kent County Council v G & Others [2005] UKHL 68), their Lordships concluded that what a court directs under s.38(6) must clearly be **an examination or assessment of the child** and that any services*

*provided for the child or her/his family must be
ancillary to that end.*

Exclusion Requirements in Interim Care Orders [s.38A (3) as inserted by s.52 & Sch.6 FLA 1996]

- Provisions described below enable the court when
  making an Interim Care Order, to attach an exclusion
  requirement so a suspected abuser can be
  removed/kept away from the home in which the
  child is living or from the surrounding area.

- Where the court is satisfied that there are reasonable
  grounds for believing the threshold criteria for Care
  and Supervision (s.31) are met, and consequently
  makes an I.C.O., the court may include an 'exclusion
  requirement' **if:**

  - It is reasonable cause to believe if a 'relevant
    person' is excluded from a dwelling-house in
    which child lives, s/he will cease to suffer/be
    likely to suffer significant harm and
  - Another person living in the same dwelling-
    house (parent or other person) is able/willing to
    give the child the care which it would be
    reasonable to expect a parent to give, and
    consents to it [s.38A as inserted by s.52 Sch.6
    FLA 1996]

- An 'exclusion requirement' is any 1 or more of the
  following provisions which may:

  - Require the relevant person to leave a dwelling-
    house in which s/he is living with the child

- Prohibit the relevant person from entering a dwelling-house in which the child lives, e.g. if the local authority places the child with a relative
- Exclude the relevant person from a defined area in which a dwelling-house is included and in which the child is situated, e.g. if the local authority places her/him with a relative

Duration of Exclusion Requirements in Interim Care Orders [s.38A (4) as inserted by s.52 & Sch.6 FLA 1996]

■ Court may provide that the exclusion requirement is to have effect for a shorter period than other provisions of an Interim Care Order.

NB. There is no power to extend exclusion requirements beyond interim or Emergency Protection Order stage. If continuing protection is sought, application must be made by person with whom child living for an injunction under s.100 or a Prohibited Steps Order.

Power of Arrest [s.38A (5) as inserted by s.52 & Sch.6 FLA 1996]

■ Exclusion requirements may have a power of arrest attached [s.38A (5) as inserted by s.52 and Sch.6 FLA 1996].

■ Where a power of arrest is attached, a court may provide it is to have effect for a shorter period than exclusion requirement.

NB. Any period specified for purpose of ss.4 or 6 above, may be extended by court on 1 or more occasion on application to vary or discharge an Interim Care Order [s.38A (7) CA 1989 inserted by s.52 and Sch.6 FLA 1996].

■ Where a power of arrest is attached to an exclusion requirement of an Interim Care Order, a constable may arrest without warrant, any person whom s/he has reasonable cause to believe is in breach of requirement [s.38A (8) as inserted by s.52 and Sch.6 FLA 1996].

■ If, while an Interim Care Order with exclusion requirements is in force, local authority has removed a child from dwelling-house from which 'relevant person' is excluded to other accommodation for continuous period of over 24, the exclusion requirement ceases [s.38A (10) as inserted by s.52 and Sch.6 FLA 1996].

Undertakings Relating To Interim Care Orders [s.38B as inserted by s.52 Sch.6 FLA 1996]

■ In any case where court has power to include an exclusion requirement in Interim Care Order, it may accept an undertaking from relevant person.

■ In such cases no power of arrest may be attached [s.38B (1) & (2) as inserted by s.52 & Sch.6 FLA 1996].

■ Such an undertaking will:

- Be enforceable as if it were an order of the court
- Cease to have effect if, whilst in force, local authority removes child from dwelling-house from which relevant person excluded, to other accommodation for a continuous period of over 24 hours [s.38B(3) CA 1989 as inserted by s.52 & Sch.6 FLA 1996]

■ On the application of a person not entitled to apply for discharge/variation of Care Order/Supervision Order, but who is a person to whom an exclusion requirement contained in the order applies, an Interim Care Order may be varied/discharged by the court in so far as it imposes the exclusion requirement [s.39 (3A) as inserted by s.52 & sch. 6 FLA 1996].

■ Where a power of arrest has been attached to an exclusion requirement of an Interim Care Order, the court may, on the application of any person entitled to apply for the discharge of the order so far as it imposes the exclusion requirement, vary or discharge the order in so far as it confers a power of arrest (regardless of whether any application has been made to vary/discharge any other provision) [s.39(3B) CA 1989 as inserted by s.52 & Sch.6 FLA 1996].

Best Practice in Care Proceedings

■ In Re E and Others (Minors) (Care Proceedings: Social Work Practice) [2000] 2 FLR 254 FD, Bracewell J issued the following guidelines:

- The top document of every social work file should be a running chronology of significant events kept up to date to facilitate identification of serious and deep rooted problems rather than the circumstances triggering the instant referral
- Lack of parental co-operation was never a reason to close a file or remove a child from a protection register (it was instead justification for more intense investigation)
- Referrals from professionals should be given great weight and investigated thoroughly
- Line managers and others with decision making power should never make a judgement to take no action without full knowledge of file and consulting those professionals who knew family
- Siblings should not be considered in isolation, but in context of family history taking account of problems and results of intervention with respect to previous children
- To avoid drift, work with families has to be time limited and require changes within time scales

EDUCATION SUPERVISION ORDERS (E.S.O.) [S.36]

Applications

- By local education authority following consultation with social services.

Grounds

- Court must be satisfied child of compulsory school age and not being properly educated (i.e. receiving efficient full-time education suitable to her/his age, ability, aptitude and any special educational needs).

NB. An Education Supervision Order may not be made for a child in care, but is possible for one who is accommodated.

Effect [Sch.3 para.12]

- Child under supervision of the local education authority and the supervisor must:

  - Advise, assist, befriend and give directions to child/parents to secure proper education
  - Consider, where directions given have not been complied with, what further steps to take

NB. Before giving directions, the supervisor must, so far as is reasonably practicable, ascertain wishes/ feelings of child/parents, in particular desired place of education.

Duration [Sch.3 para.15]

- Initially 1 year but may be extended on more than 1 occasion for up to 3 years at a time.

- Ceases if child attains school leaving age or is made subject of a Care Order.

Discharge & Variation of Care Order, Supervision Order & Education Supervision Order [ss.39; 91; Sch.3 para.17]

- Care Order by person with parental responsibility, child or local authority.

- Supervision Order by person with parental responsibility, child or supervisor.

- Education Supervision Order by child, parent or local education authority.

  NB. Where an application has been made for discharge of a Care Order, Supervision Order, no further application may be made within 6 months without the leave of the court.

Children's Guardians

- Since 01.04.01 the functions previously fulfilled by guardians-ad-litem in public law proceedings have been provided for by re-titled officers engaged by the Children and Family Courts Advisory and Support Service (CAFCASS).

- Children's guardians play an active role as representatives for the child and advisors to the court on e.g. time-tabling and directions.

Function	Title
Report by CAFCASS officer s.7(1) (a)	Children and Family Reporter
Report by local authority s.7(1) (b)	Welfare Officer
Representation of child in public law proceedings s.41	Children's Guardian
Representation of child subject in adoption case	Children's Guardian
Parental consent in adoption	Reporting Officer
Representation of child in Human Fertilisation and Embryology Act 1990 case	Parental Order Reporter

- For 'specified proceedings' (Care, Supervision, Child Assessment, Emergency Protection Orders, making or revocation of Placement Orders and making , varying or discharging s.8 orders) the court must appoint a children's guardian unless satisfied this is unnecessary [s.41 as amended by s.122 ACA 2002].

- Children's guardians have a right of access to all records concerning the child belonging to or held by the local authority or the N.S.P.C.C. [s.42 (1)].

  NB. The role of a children's guardian comes to an end with the proceedings in respect of which s/he has been appointed [Re M Prohibited Steps Order: Application for Leave FD 24.08.92].

A local authority cannot interfere with the manner in which children's guardians carry out their duties (following an attempt to impose a maximum number of hours for various reports) [R v Cornwall County Council ex parte G [1992] 1 PLR 270].

Investigation by Local Authority of Need for Care or Supervision Order [s.37]

- In any family proceedings, if the court feels a Care or Supervision Order may be necessary it can ask the local authority to investigate.

- A report of the local authority's findings should normally be provided to the court within 8 weeks [s.37 (4)].

Part V: Child Protection

Child Protection

Local Authority Duty to Make Enquiries [s.47 (1) (a) as amended by Crime & Disorder Act 1998]

■ When told a child is subject of an Emergency Protection Order (E.P.O), Police Powers of Protection (P.P.O.P.) or it has reasonable cause to suspect s/he is suffering/likely to suffer 'significant harm', or has contravened a ban imposed under the Crime and Disorder Act 1998, the local authority must make enquiries to enable a decision on any necessary action to safeguard and promote a child's welfare.

■ For the distinction between 'reasonable cause to believe' and 'reasonable cause to suspect', see R (On the Application of S) v Swindon Borough Council and Another [2001] 3 FCR 702.

NB. In the case of a curfew contravention, enquiries must be begun as soon as soon as practicable and in any case within 48 hours of the local authority receiving the information [s.47 (1) (a) (iii) as inserted by s.15 (4) CDA 1998].

■ It is the duty of a local authority, education, housing or health authority/trust, and the N.S.P.C.C. (unless unreasonable to do so) to assist these enquiries e.g. by providing relevant information/advice [s.47 (9) and (11)].

■ In Z v the UK [2001] 2 FLR 612 (formerly X v Bedfordshire CC) (HL), the European Court found failure by local authority over 4 years to respond appropriately to concerns about victims of abuse and neglect by their parents, disclosed breaches of their human rights.

■ In the above case the breaches were found to be under Articles 3 (Freedom from Inhuman or Degrading Treatment), and 13 (Right of Access to the Courts and the Right to an Effective Remedy).

*NB. It should be noted alongside the above case that in D v East Berkshire Community Health NHS Trust; MAK v Dewsbury Healthcare NHS Trust; RK v Oldham NHS Trust [2005] UKHL 23 it was found that health care and other child care professionals did **not** owe a common law duty of care to parents not to make unfounded allegations of child abuse. The child, not parent was the doctor's patient in whose best interest s/he was obliged to act.*

Provision of Accommodation to Protect Child [Sch. 2 para.5]

■ If it appears to a local authority that a child living on particular premises is suffering or is likely to suffer ill treatment at the hands of another person living there, and that other person proposes to move out, the local authority may assist her/him to obtain alternative accommodation.

EMERGENCY PROTECTION ORDERS (E.P.O.) [S.44]

Applications

■ By anyone without notice to the other parties, to a court or individual magistrate.

NB. It has already been argued in Scotland that such applications being made without notice are in breach of Article 6 (Right To a Fair Trial). Reference might also be made the 'proportionality principle' as in Re C and B (Care Order: Future Harm [2002] 1 FLR 610.

Grounds

■ The 1st possible ground is that the court must be satisfied that there is reasonable cause to believe the child is likely to suffer 'significant harm' if not removed to accommodation provided by applicant or does not remain in current location e.g. hospital [s.44 (1) (a)].

■ The 2nd possible ground is that the local authority or N.S.P.C.C. investigation of risk is being frustrated by unreasonable refusal of access [s.44 (1) (b) or (c) respectively].

*NB. Social worker or N.S.P.C.C. officer must produce identification. Early morning removal of a child is only justified where clear grounds exist that significant harm would otherwise occur or where vital evidence is obtainable only by such means [Re A (Minors) [1992] 1 All ER 153] **and** is* *proportionate to the end sought to be achieved (i.e. protection of the health of children – Articles 8(1) & (2) of the Convention).*

For the Human Rights considerations to which the use of E.P.O.s can give rise, see the decision of Munby J in X Council v B [2005] 1 FLR 341 and Langley v Liverpool City Council [2006] 1 FLR 342. In the X case it was held that the removal of the 3 younger children from the parent's home on an E.P.O. had been an inappropriate use of the order in all the circumstances of the case, whereas in Langley where the order had been used to prevent the father who was blind from driving his young children around in a car, the use of such an order was deemed to be appropriate.

Effect

■ Gives applicant parental responsibility and right to remove/prevent removal of child.

■ If, during course of an E.P.O. it appears to applicant it would be safe to return child/allow her/him to leave place of detention, applicant must do this.

■ If the child is returned home and it proves necessary (within time limit of the Emergency Protection Order the order can be re-activated.

Duration [s.45]

■ Up to 8 days with 1 possible extension up to a further 7 days.

- If the last day of an 8 day order falls on a public holiday (Christmas, Good Friday, a Bank Holiday or Sunday) the court may specify a period which ends at noon on the 1st later day which is not a public holiday.

NB. The court will consider appointment of a children's guardian at the application stage.

Exclusion Requirements in Emergency Protection Orders [s.44A as inserted by s.52 & Sch.6 FLA 1996]

■ Provisions described below enable the court when making an E.P.O. to attach an exclusion requirement so that a suspected abuser can be removed/kept away from the home in which the child is living or the surrounding area.

NB. It has already been stated that 'without notice' orders (those made when no notice has been given to the other party requiring them to attend court) may offend against Article 6. This is even more probable in attaching exclusion requirements where it may also be argued that there is a potential breach of Article 1 Protocol 1 of the Convention (Right to Peaceful Enjoyment of Possessions), in this case, one's home.

■ Where the court is satisfied that the threshold criteria for an E.P.O. are satisfied and they make such an order, it may also include an exclusion requirement **if** the following conditions are satisfied:

- There is reasonable cause to believe that if the 'relevant person' is excluded from a dwelling-house in which the child lives then the child will not be likely to suffer significant harm either if s/he is not removed (i.e. s.44(1)(a)(i), or does not remain (i.e. s.44(1)(a)(ii), or because enquiries as per s.44(1) (b) or (c) will cease to be frustrated
- Another person living in the same dwelling-house (parent or not) is able and willing to give to the child the care which it would be reasonable to give her/him and that person consents to the inclusion of the exclusion requirement.

NB. An argument could be made in respect of potential breaches of Article 8 and Article 1 Protocol 1 of the Convention, and the proportionality principle previously referred to is also relevant.

- An 'exclusion requirement' for the purposes of s.44A is any 1 or more of the following provisions:

  - Requiring the relevant person to leave a dwelling-house in which s/he is living with a child
  - Prohibiting the relevant person from entering a dwelling-house in which the child lives
  - Excluding the relevant person from a defined area in which a dwelling-house in which the child lives is situated [s.44A(5) as inserted by s.52 & Sch.6 FLA 1996]

Duration of Exclusion Requirement in Emergency Protection Order [s.44A (4) as inserted by s.52 & Sch. 6 FLA 1996]

■ The court may provide that the exclusion requirement is to have effect for a shorter period than the other provisions of the order.

NB. There is no power to extend exclusion requirements beyond interim or E.P.O. stage and if continuing protection is sought for the child an application must be made by the person with whom the child is living for an injunction under s.100 or perhaps a Prohibited Steps Order.

Power of Arrest [s.44A (5) as inserted by s.52 & Sch.6 FLA 1996]

■ The exclusion requirement may have a power of arrest attached to it [s.44A(5)] and where it does so, the court may provide that the power of arrest is to have effect for a shorter period than the exclusion requirement [s.44A(6) inserted by s.52 & Sch.6 FLA 1996].

NB. Any period specified for the purposes of ss. (4) or (6) may be extended by the court on 1 or more occasions on an application to vary or discharge the E.P.O. [s.44A (7) as inserted by s.52 & Sch.7 FLA 1996].

■ Where a power of arrest is attached to an exclusion requirement of an E.P.O. a constable may arrest without warrant any person whom s/he has reasonable grounds to believe to be in breach of the requirement [s.44A (8) inserted by s.52 & Sch.6 FLA 1996].

■ If while an E.P.O. containing an exclusion requirement is in force, the applicant has removed the child from the dwelling-house from which the relevant person is excluded, to other accommodation for a continuous period of over 24 hours, the order shall cease to have effect in so far as it imposes the exclusion requirement [s.44A (10) inserted by s.52 & Sch.6 FLA 1996].

Undertakings Relating to Emergency Protection Orders [s.44B as inserted by s.52 & Sch.6 FLA 1996]

■ In any case where the court has power to include an exclusion requirement in an E.P.O. the court may accept an undertaking from the relevant person and in such cases no power of arrest may be attached [s.44B(1) & (2) inserted by s.52 & Sch.6 FLA 1996].

■ Such an undertaking:

- Is enforceable as if it were an order of the court and
- Will cease to have effect if, whilst it is in force, the applicant has removed the child from the dwelling-house from which the relevant person is excluded to other accommodation for a continuous period of more than 24 hours [s.44B(3) inserted by s.52 & Sch.6 FLA 1996]

- On the application of a person not entitled to apply for the order to be discharged, but to whom an exclusion requirement contained in it applies, an E.P.O. may be varied or discharged by a court in so far as it imposes the exclusion requirement [s.45 (8A) as inserted by s.52 & Sch.6 FLA 1996].

- Where a power of arrest has been attached to an exclusion requirement the court may, on application of any person entitled to apply for discharge of the order so far as it imposes the exclusion requirement, vary or discharge the order in so far as it confers a power of arrest (regardless of whether any application has been made to vary or discharge any other provision [s.45 (8B) as inserted by s.52 & Sch.6 FLA 1996].

Challenge to E.P.O.

- 72 hours after an E.P.O. is made, an application for discharge can be made by parent, person with parental responsibility, child or anyone with whom s/he was living at time order made.

  NB. Restricting the right to apply for 72 hours may be a potential infringement of the rights contained in Article 6 (Right To a Fair Trial).

  Reasonable contact is assumed between child and above parties. Court may be asked for/may give directions to limit contact and/or about medical/psychiatric examinations. If of sufficient understanding a child may refuse examination.

Discovery [s.48 (1)]

■ If necessary, a court may direct someone to disclose to an applicant for an E.P.O., the whereabouts of a child.

NB. A statement or admission made in complying with a court direction to disclose a child's whereabouts is not admissible in evidence against person or spouse in proceedings other than perjury.

Entry/ Search [s.48 (3)]

■ An E.P.O. may also include directions to enter and search (but not by force).

Warrant [s.48 (9) & (10)]

■ Where a court believes applicant has been/is likely to be refused access to child it may issue a warrant to police to assist, using if necessary, reasonable force.

NB. Court can direct that police be accompanied by a doctor, nurse or health visitor.

POLICE POWER OF PROTECTION (P.P.O.P.) [S.46]

Grounds [s.46 (1)]

■ Police must have reasonable grounds to believe child would otherwise suffer 'significant harm'.

NB. Police powers of protection may arguably breach Article 8(1) (Right to Respect for Private and Family Life). Although qualified by reference to Article 8(2) which describes the circumstances in which a public authority is allowed to interfere with this right, the 'proportionality principle' [see above] will still apply.

Where an E.P.O. is in force, s.46 should only be invoked where it is impracticable to execute it, having regard to the paramount need to protect children from significant harm (see Langley v Liverpool City Council [2006] 1 FLR 342 above at p 135.)

Effect

■ Police powers of protection:

- Allow a police constable to remove and accommodate child or
- Ensure that s/he remains in current location
- Do not give parental responsibility
- Do allow police to do all that is reasonable

Duration [s.46 (6)]

■ Up to 72 hours.

Conditions

■ Police must inform parent, local authority and child of steps taken [s.46 (3) and (4)], and

■ Transfer her/him as soon as possible to local authority accommodation, though the responsibility for ongoing enquiries and any decision to release child from police protection remains with the police.

NB. Police can also apply for an E.P.O. to be made in favour of a local authority. If so, any time spent in police protection must be deducted from duration of the E.P.O.

Recovery Order [s.50] Applications

■ Local authority, N.S.P.C.C. and police if child subject of Emergency Protection or Care Order (including Interim Care Order)

■ Police if subject of police protection.

Grounds

■ Child subject to Care Order, an E.P.O. or in police protection, and:

  • Has run away or
  • Is being kept away from a responsible person who should be caring for her/him, or
  • Is missing

Effect

■ Directs responsible person to produce child or to inform of whereabouts.

■ Authorises police to search (using reasonable force if necessary), and

■ Allows removal of child by authorised person.

Refuges [s.51]

■ If foster carers, private or voluntary homes have a certificate from the Secretary of State they are exempt from the law covering abduction of children.

NB. Re: R (Recovery Order) [1998] 2 FLR 401 concerned a boy with behavioural difficulties subject of a Care Order placed at a residential school during term time and with mother in the holidays. The court held that the local authority was entitled to designate both the head teacher in term time and the mother in the holidays as the 'responsible person'. When the boy refused to return to school the local authority could obtain a s.50 Order, replace without notice and cite the mother and head teacher as the responsible persons if the boy's welfare required it.

CHILD ASSESSMENT ORDER (C.A.O.) [S.43]

Applications

■ By local authority or N.S.P.C.C. [s.43 (1)].

NB. Applicant must provide 7 days notice to persons listed in s.43(11) and a court can treat the application as if it were for an E.P.O. and make such an order instead [s.43(3)].

Grounds [s.43 (1)]

■ Applicant must satisfy the court that s/he has reasonable cause to suspect child is suffering or is likely to suffer 'significant harm' and

- Needs an assessment of state of child's health or development or way in which s/he has been treated to determine if suffering or likely to suffer 'significant harm', and
- Assessment is otherwise unlikely to be undertaken or to be satisfactory

NB. 'Reasonable cause to suspect' is a much lower threshold than 'reasonable cause to believe' held the court in R (on the Application of S) v Swindon Borough Council and Another [2001] 3 FCR 702.

Effect [s.43 (6)]

■ Obliges person/s to produce child and comply with court directions e.g. a medical and any other form of assessment – see Re C [1997] 1 FLR 1 [HL].

NB. If of sufficient understanding or aged 16 or over, a child may refuse a medical.

If necessary a child who is subject of a C.A.O. may be kept from home.

Duration [s.43 (6)]

■ From a specified date and for such period, not exceeding 7 days, which may be specified.

Rights of Refusal of Medical & Other Assessment [ss.38; 43; 44]

■ The child's right to refuse medical, psychiatric or dental investigations is limited to the assessment stages of the order provided for in above sections.

NB. For circumstances in which the child's refusal may be overruled, see South Glamorgan CC v W and B [1993] 1 FLR 574 where High Court's inherent jurisdiction under s.100 Children Act 1989 was invoked to override the refusal of a 15 year old refusal of a psychiatric assessment in an interim Care Order s.38(6) direction.

Parts VI–XII: Homes, Childminding etc

Registration & Inspection Duties

PRIVATE FOSTERING [PART IX]

Definition [s.66]

- Child under 16 (18 if disabled) and cared for and accommodated by non-relative, or someone without parental responsibility for over 27 days.

Requirements [Sch.8 and relevant regulations]

- Foster carer must notify local authority.

- Local authority has a duty to inspect [s.67].

  NB. Unless siblings or local authority grants exemption, there is a 'usual fostering limit' of 3 children (i.e. 4 or more becomes a Children's Home).

Voluntary and Private Homes [Part VII & VIII]

- Voluntary and private homes have similar duties to local authorities [ss.61&64].

- The Commission for Social Care Inspection (CSCI) and the National Assembly (in Wales) are accountable for inspection (Care Standards Act 2000).

Childminding & Day Care Registration and Inspection [Part XA]

- Part XA (introduced by Part VI of the Care Standards Act 2000) describes responsibilities for registration and inspection of childminding and all types of group care which :

- In England are the responsibility of Her Majesty's Inspectorate of School (operating through the Early Years Directorate of Ofsted) and
- In Wales, the responsibility of the Care Standards Inspectorate

NB. The role of the local authority is the supply of information, advice and training.

Definitions [s.79A]

- A 'childminder' is someone, other than a parent, relative, person with parental responsibility, or foster parent, who looks after one or more children aged under 8, in domestic premises for over 2 hours a day, for reward.

- 'Day care' is care/supervised activity provided for a child under 8 in daytime on non-domestic premises for over 2 hours a day.

Registration, De-Registration and Cancellation of Registration [s.79C-M introduced by Part VI Care Standards Act 2000]

- Persons offering minding or day care must apply to register with the relevant registration authority.

- Legislation covering childcare provision and regulation is changing. The 'Childcare Act 2006' when implemented, is intended to assist in implementation of the aims set out in *'Choice for Parents, the Best Start for Children: a Ten Year Strategy for Childcare'* (HMSO 2004) which set out the Government's plans for the future of childcare.

NB. CAE plans to produce a guide to the above law in early 2007.

Miscellaneous & General [Part XII]

Notification to Local Authority of Certain Children by Health/ Education/ Residential Care, Nursing & Mental Nursing Homes [ss.85; 86]

■ If above organisations do, or plan to accommodate child for 12 weeks or more, they must notify the local authority.

■ The local authority must take reasonable steps to determine if child's welfare is adequately safeguarded and promoted.

Independent Schools [s.87 (1)-(5) as amended by s.105 Care Standards Act 2000]

■ When such schools accommodate children, they must safeguard and promote their welfare.

■ CSCI (or in Wales the National Assembly) has a duty to check this and a right to enter premises at any reasonable time.

Youth Justice [s.90; Sch.12]

■ Care Order for criminal behaviour abolished

■ Amendments to Children and Young Persons Act 1969 means the court can in certain circumstances impose a 'residence requirement' on the subject of a 'criminal' S.O. to live in local authority accommodation

Admissibility of Child's Evidence [s.96]

■ If court believes child does not understand nature of oath her/his evidence may still be heard if, in court's opinion:

- Child does understand s/he has a duty to tell the truth, and
- S/he has sufficient understanding to justify evidence being heard

■ The child's statement or a statement by another person concerning the upbringing, maintenance or welfare of the child is admissible (notwithstanding the normal hearsay rule).

■ Hearsay evidence is admissible in all Children Act proceedings in a magistrates' court including an application for a Secure Accommodation Order [R.(J.) v. Oxfordshire County Council [1992] All ER 660] and presumably an application for an E.P.O.

Self Incrimination [s.98]

■ In any proceedings in which a court is hearing an application for an order under Part IV or V of the Children Act 1989, no person is excused (on the grounds that doing so might incriminate her/him or spouse) from:

- Giving evidence on any matter
- Answering any question put in the course of giving evidence

■ A statement or admission made in such proceedings

shall not be admissible in evidence against the person making it or spouse in proceedings for an offence other than perjury.

NB. See Re C [1996] 2 FLR 725 and Re M (Care Proceedings: Disclosure) [2001] 2 FLR 1316

Police Investigation: Privilege

■ The House of Lords affirmed in Re L (Police Investigation: Privilege) [1996] 1 FLR 731 HL, that:

- In proceedings under the Act the better view is that no privilege attaches to expert reports or indeed to anything except direct solicitor/client communications and
- Accordingly, the present practice of requiring disclosure as a condition of obtaining leave for expert evidence is proper.

NB. The above decision of the House of Lords is reinforced by Article 6 (Right To A Fair Trial) which encompasses the notion of full disclosure to all parties of all relevant documents.

Courts: Functions & Structures

Youth Courts

- Jurisdiction limited to criminal matters.

- Age range 10 to 17 years inclusive.

Family Proceedings Courts

- Most public law cases start and many are dealt with entirely at this level of (specially trained) family panel magistrates.

  NB. Magistrates must give reasons for decisions in all cases (interim as well as final), set out relevant facts in chronological order or under convenient headings, make clear which facts were disputed and any findings made on them and also indicate the factors (even when obvious) used in balancing exercise which enabled them to arrive at decisions. A standard format exists for this purpose.

- The Children Act Advisory Committee in 1993/94 report (p. 50) stated magistrates are capable of hearing straightforward cases lasting up to 4 or 5 days, provided they are able to sit on consecutive days and there are no complex issues involved.

Care Centres

- Full family law jurisdiction including public law cases transferred from Family Proceedings Court.

■ Public law cases heard by 'nominated' Care Judges in any Care Centre.

NB. Public law cases can begin at County Court level if a judge has given a s.37 direction or public law proceedings are already pending in County Court.

Family Hearing Centres

■ Full private family law jurisdiction.

■ Circuit Family Judges deal with contested applications.

Divorce County Court

■ Deals with uncontested s.8 applications; arrangements for children except if divorce defended or arrangements contested; uncontested adoptions.

Non-Divorce County Court

■ Domestic violence/matrimonial injunctions only, though within these proceedings Circuit & District Judges can make interim s.8 orders.

NB. Adoptions may only be made in Divorce County Courts, Care or Family Hearing Centres

High Court

■ Family Judges in Family Division of High Court.

Hearings

- As a result of the relevant clause in Article 6 (Right To A Fair Trial), judgement must be pronounced publicly although Press and public may be excluded from all or part of the trial in the interests of e.g. morals, or where interests of juveniles or protection of private life of the parties so require [for remaining issues, see Article 6(1)].

- Pursuant to s.62 CA 2004, guidance has been issued to all Family Judges that they are now required in accordance with the section and with Articles 6 and 10 to issue judgements in open court, though as with Court of Appeal, expected to anonymise all personal details which might lead to identification of any of the parties.

- In B v UK (Hearing in Private) 2000 FLR 97(application number 36337/97), the European Court ruled a father's application to have a Residence Order hearing in public should be heard by the European Court of Human Rights as a potential breach of Article 6 – that court hearings **should** be heard in public. The Court also found a potential breach under Article 10 (Right to Receive and Impart Information) in that he was not allowed to divulge information concerning the proceedings.

Transfer of Cases

- Lateral transfers are possible between Family Proceedings Courts and between County Courts

when deemed to be in child's best interests because
of:

- A need to avoid delay
- A need to consolidate with other family
  proceedings, or
- For some other reason

■ Vertical transfer from Family Proceedings to County
Court is possible when deemed to be in best
interests of child if case:

- Is exceptionally grave, important or complex;
- Should be heard with other Family Proceedings
- Requires accelerated determination

■ Transfer from County Court to High Court is possible
if the former considers the proceedings to be more
suitable for hearing there, e.g. a precedent to be set,
major principle involved, in best interests of the
child.

■ Transfer down from the High Court to County Court
possible to enable consolidation with other
proceedings.

■ Family Proceedings cases estimated to last in excess
of two (at most three) days should be considered for
transfer to a higher court, as should cases involving
conflicting expert evidence or need to evaluate
future risk of harm to children [Essex County Council
v L The Times 18/12/92 FD and Re S 20/7/92
unreported FD].

Court Structures

- Full-time District Judges are allowed to make the following orders:

  - Private Law – upon application under s.10, an Order limited in time for Residence and Contact; upon application under s.13(1) to remove children from the jurisdiction an order limited in time (e.g. removal for purpose of holiday/family visit) and upon a reference under s.16 by a Children and Family Reporter, an Order to vary a s.8 Order when a Family Assistance Order is in force
  - Public Law – under s.38, an Interim Care or Supervision Order and under s.38A, an Exclusion Order

- All these orders will be limited in time until the next hearing, and made returnable before a Circuit Judge at the expiry of the period.

  NB. The government in June 2003 announced its intention to introduce changes that would mean a 'Supreme Court fulfilling the functions currently fulfilled by the House of Lords' Law Lords and represented over-leaf. This has not yet been implemented.

Court Structures

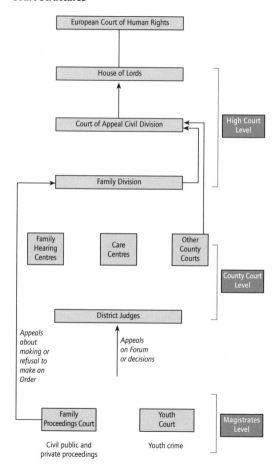

Appendices

Appendix 1: Convention Rights and Fundamental Freedoms [Articles 2–12 and 14 of Convention, Articles 1–3 First Protocol and Articles 1 and 2 Sixth Protocol, as read with Articles 16–18 of Convention]

With effect from 02.10.00, all courts in England and Wales have been required, so far as is possible to interpret all legislation, whenever enacted, in a way which is compatible with the European Convention on Human Rights.

It is unlawful for public authorities to act in a way which is incompatible with Convention rights summarised in the following pages.

When introducing legislation, government must make a statement about the compatibility of the Bill with Convention rights.

> *'The HRA 1998 is the most significant statement of human rights in the UK since the 1689 Bills of Rights (a statement by the then Home Office Minister Paul Boateng 26.11.99).*

Article 2 – Right to Life

Everyone's right to life shall be protected by law and no one shall be deprived of her/his life intentionally except in the execution of a sentence of a court following her/his conviction of a crime for which this penalty is provided in law.

This Article is not contravened if force, no more than absolutely necessary is used:

a) In defence of any person from unlawful violence

b) In order to effect a lawful arrest or to prevent the escape of a person lawfully detained

c) In action lawfully taken for the purpose of quelling a riot or insurrection

Relevant cases: Osman v UK [1999] 1 FLR 193, Keenan v UK (21 May 2001) EHRR 2001.

Article 3 – Prohibition of Torture

No one shall be subjected to torture or to inhuman or degrading treatment or punishment.

Relevant case: A v UK [1998] 2 FLR 959.

Article 4 – Prohibition of Slavery and Forced Labour

No one shall be held in slavery or servitude.

No one shall be required to perform forced or compulsory labour.

'Forced' or 'compulsory' labour excludes work required in the ordinary course of detention in accordance with Article 5 [see below] or during

conditional release from such detention; any military service or its equivalent for conscientious objectors; any service exacted in the case of an emergency or calamity which threatens life or well being of the community; any work or service which forms part of normal civic obligations.

Article 5 – Right to Liberty & Security

1. Everyone has the right to liberty and security of person. No one shall be deprived of liberty except in the following cases and in accordance with a procedure described in law:

   a) Lawful detention of a person after conviction by a competent court.

   b) Lawful arrest or detention of a person for non-compliance with the lawful order of a court or in order to secure the fulfilment of any obligation prescribed below.

   c) Lawful arrest or detention to bring a person before the competent legal authority on reasonable suspicion of having committed an offence (or when it is reasonably considered necessary to prevent her/him committing an offence or from fleeing having done so).

   d) Detention of a minor by lawful order for purpose of educational supervision or lawful detention so as to bring her/him before the competent legal authority.

   e) Lawful detention of persons for the prevention of the spreading of infectious diseases, of

persons of unsound mind, alcoholics, drug
addicts or vagrants.

f) Lawful arrest or detention of a person to prevent
her/him effecting an unauthorised entry into
the country or of a person against whom action
is being taken with a view to deportation or
extradition.

2. Everyone who is arrested must be informed promptly
in a language s/he understands of the reasons and
of any charges against them.

3. Everyone arrested/detained in accordance with
para.1.c). above, must be brought promptly before a
judge or another officer authorised by law to
exercise judicial power and is entitled to trial within
a reasonable period of time, or release pending trial
or release may be conditioned by guarantees to
appear for trial.

4. Everyone who is deprived of liberty by
arrest/detention is entitled to take proceedings by
which the lawfulness of her/his detention is decided
speedily by a court and release ordered if the
detention is not lawful.

5. Everyone who has been the victim of
arrest/detention in contravention of the provisions
of this Article has an enforceable right to
compensation.

Article 6 – Right to Fair Trial

1. In the determination of her/his civil rights and

obligations or of any criminal charge against them, everyone is entitled to a fair and public hearing within a reasonable time by an independent and impartial tribunal established by law. Judgement must be given publicly but the press and public may be excluded from all or part of the trial in the interests of morals, public order or national security in a democratic society; where the interests of juveniles or the protection of the private life of the parties require it; or to the extent strictly necessary in the court's opinion in special circumstances where publicity would prejudice the interests of justice.

2. Everyone charged with a criminal offence must be presumed innocent until proved guilty according to law.

3. Everyone charged with a criminal offence has the following minimum rights:

   a) To be informed promptly in a language s/he understands in detail of the nature and reason for the accusation.
   b) To have adequate time and facilities for preparation of defence.
   c) To defend her/himself in person or through legal assistance of the person's choosing, or if of insufficient means to pay for legal assistance to be given it free when the interests of justice require it.
   d) To examine or have examined witnesses against her/him and to obtain the attendance and examination of witnesses on her/his behalf

> under the same conditions as witnesses against her/him.

e) To have the free assistance of an interpreter if s/he cannot understand or speak the language used in court.

Relevant case: Re A (Separate Representation) [2001] 1 FLR 715 and Re M (Care: Challenging Decision by a Local Authority) [2001] 2 FLR 1300.

Article 7 – No Punishment without Law

1. No one must be held guilty of any criminal offence on account of any act or omission which did not constitute a criminal offence under national or international law at the time when it was committed. Nor must a heavier penalty be imposed than the one which was applicable at the time the criminal offence was committed.

2. This Article must not prejudice the trial and punishment of any person for any act or omission which at the time it was committed was criminal according to the general principles of law recognised by civilised nations.

Article 8 – Right to Respect for Private & Family Life

1. Everyone has the right to respect for her/his private and family life, home and correspondence.

2. There must be no interference by a public authority with the exercise of this right except such as is in

accordance with the law and is necessary in a democratic society in the interests of national security, public safety or the economic well being of the country, for the prevention of disorder or crime, for the protection of health or morals, or for the protection of the rights and freedoms of others.

Relevant cases: Hendrik v Netherlands [1982] 5 EHRR 223 – children's interests will always prevail over parents' rights to private and family life endorsed in Dawson v Wearmouth [1999] 1 FLR 1167 and reported by Court of Appeal in Re L, V, M and H [2000] 2 FLR 334 when Butler-Sloss stated 'in particular, the parent cannot be entitled under Article 8 of the Convention to have such measures taken as would harm child's health and development'.

Article 9 – Freedom of Thought, Conscience & Religion

1. Everyone has the right to freedom of thought, conscience and religion; this freedom includes freedom to change religion or belief and freedom either alone or in community with others and in public or in private, to manifest her/his religion or belief in worship, teaching, practice and observance.

2. Freedom to manifest one's religion or beliefs shall be subject to such limitations as are prescribed by law and are necessary in a democratic society in the interests of public safety, for the protection of public order, health or morals, or for the protection of the rights and freedoms of others.

Relevant case: Re J (Muslim Circumcision Specific Issue Order) [2000] 1 FLR 571.

Article 10 – Freedom of Expression

1. Everyone has the right of freedom of expression. This right shall include freedom to hold opinions and to receive and impart information and ideas without interference by public authority and regardless of frontiers. This Article shall not prevent States from requiring the licensing of broadcasting, television or cinema enterprises.

2. The exercise of these freedoms, since it carries with it duties and responsibilities may be subject to such formalities, conditions, restrictions or penalties as are prescribed by law and are necessary in a democratic society in the interest of national security, territorial integrity or public safety, for the protection of disorder or crime, for the protection of health or morals, for the protection of the reputation or rights of others, for preventing the disclosure of information received in confidence or for maintaining the authority and impartiality of the judiciary.

Article 11 – Freedom of Assembly & Association

1. Everyone has the right to freedom of peaceful assembly and to freedom of association with others including the right to form and join trades unions for the protection of her/his interests.

2. No restrictions shall be placed on the exercise of these rights other than such as are prescribed by law an are necessary in a democratic society in the interests of national security or public safety, for the prevention of disorder or crime or for the protection of the rights and freedoms of others. This Article shall not prevent the imposition of lawful restrictions on the exercise of these rights by members of the armed forces, of the police or of the administration of the State.

Article 12 – Right to Marry

Men and women of marriageable age have the right to marry and to found a family according to the national laws governing the exercise of that right.

Article 14 – Prohibition of Discrimination

The enjoyment of the rights and freedoms set forth in this Convention shall be secured without discrimination on any ground such as sex, race, colour, language, religion, political or other opinion, national or social origin, association with a national minority, property, birth or other status.

Breach of Article 14 cannot be argued on its own but must be linked with some other breach of a Convention Article e.g. Breach of Right To A Fair Trial' such as an argument that denying children rights to representation in residence and contact proceedings is based on discrimination on the grounds of age (Articles 6 and 14.)

ARTICLES 1–3 FIRST PROTOCOL

Article 1 – Protection of Property

Every natural or legal person is entitled to the peaceful enjoyment of their possessions. No one shall be deprived of their possessions except in the public interest and subject to conditions provided for by law and the general principles of international law (this does not impair the right of the State to enforce necessary laws on use of property or to secure payment of taxes or other contributions or penalties).

Article 2 – Right to Education

No person shall be denied the right to education. In the exercise of any functions which it assumes in relation to education and teaching, the State shall respect the rights of parents to ensure such education and teaching in conformity with their own religious and philosophical convictions.

Article 3 – Right to Free Elections

Signatory States undertake to hold free elections at reasonable intervals by secret ballot under conditions which will ensure the free expression of the opinion of the people in the choice of the legislature.

ARTICLES 1 & 2 SIXTH PROTOCOL

Article 1 – Abolition of Death Penalty

The death penalty shall be abolished. No one shall be condemned to such penalty or executed.

Article 2 – Death Penalty in time of War

A State may make provision in its law for the death penalty in respect of acts committed in time of war or of its imminent threat (such a penalty must be applied in accordance with a national law and the State must communicate the relevant provision to the Secretary General of the Council of Europe).

> *NB. All the above rights and freedoms must be read with Articles 16–18 of the Convention which are as follows.*

ARTICLES 16–18 CONVENTION RIGHTS & FREEDOMS

Article 16 – Restrictions on Political Activity of Aliens

Nothing in Articles 10, 11 &14 shall be regarded as preventing the signatories from imposing restrictions on the political activity of aliens.

Article 17 – Prohibition of Abuse of Rights

Nothing in this Convention may be interpreted as implying for any State, group or person any right to engage in any activity or perform any act aimed at the destruction of any of the rights and freedoms set forth herein, or at their limitation to a greater extent than is provided for in the Convention.

Article 18 – Limitation on Use of Restriction of Rights

Restrictions permitted under this Convention to the said rights and freedoms shall not be applied for any purpose other than those for which they have been prescribed.

Designated Derogation and Reservation

Convention Articles summarised in preceding pages are to have effect for the purposes of HRA 1998, subject to any:

- **'Designated Derogation'** [time limited capacity for the Secretary of State to suspend either Article 5(3) (arrest and detention under right to liberty and security) or any other specified Article or Protocol] [s.14 HRA 1998], or

- **'Designated Reservation'** [i.e. the UK's reservation about the Education provision implied by Protocol 1 Article 2, second sentence which is elaborated upon in Part 11 of Sch.3] [s.15 HRA 1998] or

- **Other reservation** set out in an order made by the Secretary of State.

    The Secretary of State may be order make such amendments to this Act as s/he considers appropriate to reflect the effect, in relation to the UK of a Protocol to the convention which the UK has ratified or has signed with a view to ratification [s.1(4) &(5)]. No amendment may be made by such an order so as to come into force before the Protocol concerned is in force in the UK [s.1 (6)].

Appendix 2: Human Rights Act 1998

Interpretation of Convention Rights [s.2 HRA 1998]

■ A court or tribunal determining a question which has arisen in connection with a Convention right must take into account in accordance with rules, any relevant judgement, decision, declaration or advisory opinion of the European Court of Human Rights, opinion or decision formally provided by the Commission or any decision made by the Committee of Ministers.

Interpretation of Legislation [s.3 HRA 1998]

■ So far as it is possible to do so, primary and subordinate legislation must be read and given effect in a way which is compatible with Convention rights.

■ The above provision applies:

- Whenever the primary and subordinate legislation was enacted and
- Does not affect validity, continuing operation or enforcement of any incompatible primary legislation and
- Does not affect the validity, continuing operation or enforcement of any incompatible subordinate legislation if (disregarding any

possibility of revocation) primary legislation prevents removal of the incompatibility.

Declaration of Incompatibility [s.4 HRA 1998]

■ If a court determines that the provision of primary or subordinate legislation is incompatible with a Convention right, it may make a declaration of that incompatibility [s.4 (1)–(3) HRA 1998].

NB. Court in this section means House of Lords, Judicial Committee of the Privy Council, Courts Martial Appeal Court and in England and the High Court or the Court of Appeal [s.4(5) HRA 1998]

■ A declaration of incompatibility:

- Does not affect the validity, continuing operation or enforcement of the provision in respect of which it is given and
- Is not binding on the parties to the proceedings in which it is made [s.4(6) HRA 1998]

NB. Where a court is considering whether to make a declaration of incompatibility, the Crown is entitled to notice in accordance with rules of court and may be joined as a party to the proceedings [s.5 HRA 1998].

Act of Public Authorities [s.6 (1) HRA 1998]

■ It is unlawful for a 'public authority' to act in a way which is incompatible with a Convention right

NB. A public authority includes a court or tribunal and any person certain of whose functions are functions of a public nature, but does not include either House of Parliament or a person exercising functions in connection with proceedings in Parliament.

■ A person who claims that a public authority has acted (or proposes to act) in a way which is made unlawful by s.6(1) may:

- Bring proceedings against the authority under this Act in the appropriate court or tribunal or
- Rely on the Convention right/s concerned in any legal proceedings,
- But only if s/he is (or would be) a victim of the unlawful act [s.7 (1)].

NB. Time limits do or may, in accordance with rules of court be applied to bringing such proceedings [s.1(5)] which may only be brought exercising a right of appeal on an application for judicial review or in such courts may be prescribed in rules [s.9(1)].

Power to Take Remedial Action [s.10 HRA 1998]

■ If a provision of legislation has been declared to be incompatible with a Convention right and:

- All those eligible to appeal confirm in writing that they do not intend to do so, the time limit has expired or an appeal initiated has been determined or
- The Crown determines that to achieve

compatibility with European Convention obligations, primary or secondary legislation needs amending

- A Minister of the Crown may by order make such amendments as s/he considers necessary

Freedom of Thought, Conscience & Religion [s.13 HRA 1998]

■ If a court (including a tribunal) determines that any question arising under this Act might affect the exercise by a religious organisation (itself or its members collectively) of the Convention right to freedom of thought, conscience and religion it must have particular regard to the importance of that right.

Parliamentary Statement of Compatibility [s.19 HRA 1998]

■ A Minister of the Crown in charge of a Bill in either House of Parliament must before second reading of that Bill:

- Make a written statement to the effect that the Bill's provisions are compatible with the Convention's rights or
- Make a written statement to the effect that although s/he is unable to make a statement of compatibility, the government nevertheless wishes to proceed with the Bill.

Appendix 3: CAE Publications

- Personal Guides:
    - Children Act 1989 in the Context of the Human Rights Act 1998
    - Children Act 2004 (England and Wales)
    - Child Protection
    - 'How Old Do I Have To Be... ?' (a simple guide to the rights and responsibilities of 0–21 year olds)
    - Residential Care of Children
    - Fostering
    - Crime and Disorder Act 1998
    - Sexual Offences Act 2003
    - Anti Social Behaviour
    - Domestic Violence
    - Looking After Children: Good Parenting, Good Outcomes (DH LAC System)

Available from: 103 Mayfield Road South Croydon Surrey CR2 0BH tel: 020 8651 0554 fax: 020 8405 8483 email: childact@dial.pipex.com

www.caeuk.org

Discounts for orders of 50 or more of any one title

Subject Index